McDougal, Littell
SPELLING

Aqua Level

Dolores Boylston Bohen
Assistant Superintendent
Fairfax County Public Schools
Fairfax County, Virginia

Mary Johanna Lincoln Huycke
Elementary Teacher and Reading Specialist
Fairfax County, Virginia

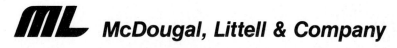 **McDougal, Littell & Company**

Evanston, Illinois
New York   Dallas   Sacramento   Raleigh

Objectives

- to teach the spelling of **words** as well as the spelling of sounds
- to stress the recognition of **structural** similarities as well as phonetic similarities
- to strengthen **associative** and **visual memory**
- to reinforce the **three modes of learning:** visual, auditory, and kinesthetic

Organization

Each lesson presents a word list that demonstrates one spelling pattern or generalization. The list is followed by three types of activities:

Practice the Words—three activities that require students to examine and write the words on the spelling list

Build Word Power—an activity that extends the application of words on the spelling list in a broader language arts context

Reach Out for New Words—two activities in which students work with new words that follow the spelling pattern

CONSULTANTS FOR THIS TEXT

Georgene G. Albert, Teacher, Pine Tree Independent School District, Longview, Texas
Carol Ashby, Teacher, Irvine Unified School District, Irvine, California
Naomi Engstrom, Teacher, Ukiah Unified School District, Ukiah, California
Lura M. Hoover, Teacher, Lakeland Community School Corporation, Milford, Indiana
Andrew L. Olson, Teacher, School District of Chetek, Chetek, Wisconsin
Mildred Seco, Teacher, North Fork School District, Glen Morgan, West Virginia
Deborah Siegler, Teacher, Jefferson Public Schools, Jefferson, Wisconsin
Wanda Travis, Teacher, Grant School District, Maysville, West Virginia
Win Yapp, Teacher, Scotts Valley Unified Elementary School District 408, Scotts Valley, California

Acknowledgments: See page 205

ISBN 0-8123-5423-0

91 92 93 / 15 14 13 12 11 10 9 8 7 6 5

Contents

A Writer's Journal

Spelling Is for Writing

Imagine that you need to write about a play at your school. What would happen if you could not spell any of the words that you wanted to write?

You learn to spell in order to write. You write to express your feelings and ideas. This book will help you improve both your spelling and your writing. The more you practice both skills, the better speller and writer you will become.

One fun way to practice writing is to keep a journal. A journal is a notebook in which you write about your thoughts and feelings. You can write whatever comes to mind.

Plan now to keep a journal throughout the year. Write in your journal often. On some days you might write only a sentence or two. On other days you may write several pages. Here are some ways you can use your journal. You can

- tell about your feelings
- remember important events in your life
- describe what you have seen or imagined
- react to a poem or story you have read

Spelling and Your Journal

When you write in your journal, you may want to use words that you do not know how to spell. Do not stop writing. Instead, write the words as you think they should be spelled. When you are finished, look up the correct spellings in the dictionary. Keep a personal list of the words that give you trouble. You can refer to this list when you need to write the words in the future.

Getting Started

Here's an idea for your first journal entry. Finish the sentence "I feel _____ today because . . ."

Building a Personal Word List

What Is a Personal Word List?

You will use your spelling book to learn how to spell many words. You will also learn important ideas about how words are spelled in our language. In this way, the spelling book helps you become a better writer. There will be times, however, when you misspell a word or need to write a word that you do not know how to spell. These words can go on a special list called a personal word list. This list will contain words that you want to learn.

Words for your personal list can come from anywhere. Many of the words will come from your writing; others may come from books you read. Here are other places you might discover words:

- stories and poems you write
- readings in content areas such as science or social studies
- signs and advertisements

How to Keep a Personal Word List

Your personal words should be kept in a special place. You might want to write the words in the back of your journal or in a special notebook. It is important to keep your list handy so that you can add words to it and refer to the list easily.

As you collect words, notice the kinds of spelling mistakes you make. Think about the way the words are spelled. Are any of the words similar to words you know how to spell? Are they made up of spelling patterns you have studied? Noticing similarities can help you remember how words are spelled.

Making Words Your Own

Making a word your own means that you can use the word correctly in your writing. To do this, you will need to know what the word means and how to spell it. A dictionary can help you with the meaning and spelling. However, you will want to develop a way of learning to spell words. One method you can use is on page 7.

How to Spell a Word

Each week you will be learning to spell a new list of words. You will also be learning words from your personal list. You will need a system—or strategy—for studying these words. One way to learn to spell a word is explained below. You can use it as you prepare for your weekly spelling test and as you learn to spell words on your personal list.

1. Look at the word.

2. Say the word.

3. Spell the word aloud.

4. Copy the word.

5. Picture the word in your mind.

6. Cover the word and write it.

   Check for mistakes. If you have made a mistake, repeat steps 1 through 6.

Silent e words with the ending ing

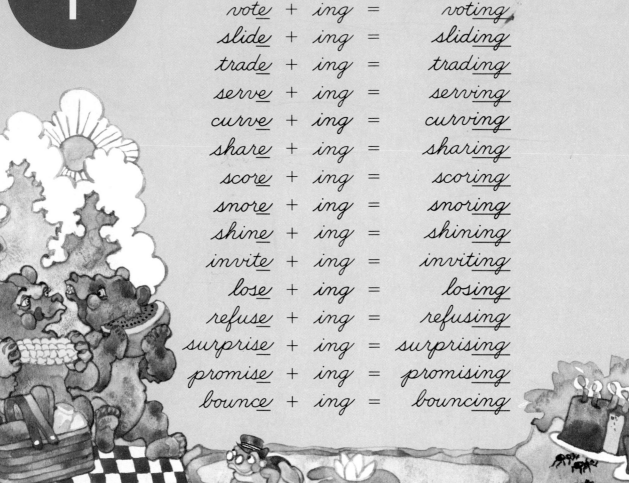

vote + ing = voting

slide + ing = sliding

trade + ing = trading

serve + ing = serving

curve + ing = curving

share + ing = sharing

score + ing = scoring

snore + ing = snoring

shine + ing = shining

invite + ing = inviting

lose + ing = losing

refuse + ing = refusing

surprise + ing = surprising

promise + ing = promising

bounce + ing = bouncing

1. What is the last letter you see in the word **vote**?
2. What is the last letter you hear in the word **vote**?
3. The words in the first column have a last letter that cannot be heard. What is that silent letter?
4. What ending was added to make the words in the last column?
5. The letters **a**, **e**, **i**, **o**, and **u** are **vowels**.
   Is the first letter of the ending **ing** a vowel?
6. What letter was dropped from each word before **ing** was added?

When a word ends with **silent e**, drop the **e** before
you add an ending that begins with a vowel.

Practice the Words

A Write the spelling words that complete these sentences.

1. Who keeps ____ the ball against the house?
2. We will be ____ dessert soon.
3. Whom is Michelle ____ to the party?
4. Rosa is ____ more points than Bill.
5. We will be ____ for a club president tomorrow.
6. Ben is ____ his apple for Sarah's grapes.
7. The police officer was ____ her flashlight into the dark alley.
8. The runner is ____ into second base.
9. Thank you for ____ your popcorn with me.
10. Ken keeps ____ to return my sweater, but he forgets.
11. Our baseball team was ____ the championship game.
12. The horse kept ____ to obey its rider.

The **base form** of a word is the word before any changes have been made.

B Unscramble the base form of each spelling word and write it. The first letter has been given to help you. Then write the **ing** form of each word.

1. tenivi _____ *i*
2. sproime _____ *p*
3. cunobe _____ *b*
4. senhi _____ *s*
5. fuseer _____ *r*
6. sprusire _____ *s*
7. creuv _____ *c*
8. neros _____ *s*

9

C Add the missing vowels to complete each spelling word. Then write its base form.

1. r _e_ f _u_ s _i_ n g   _refuse_

2. s __ r p r __ s __ n g

3. v __ t __ n g

4. s h __ r __ n g

5. s l __ d __ n g

6. p r __ m __ s __ n g

7. s __ r v __ n g

8. c __ r v __ n g

9. l __ s __ n g

10. t r __ d __ n g

11. s n __ r __ n g

12. s c __ r __ n g

Build Word Power

Writing

Write a sentence to answer each question. Use the **ing** form of the word in parentheses.

1. What are the boys doing outside?   (bounce)

2. What kind of weather are we having today?   (shine)

3. Whom is Mark asking to his party?   (invite)

4. How are the Tigers doing in the game?   (lose)

5. What are we doing for Jan's birthday?   (surprise)

voting	serving	scoring	inviting	surprising
sliding	curving	snoring	losing	promising
trading	sharing	shining	refusing	bouncing

New Words

prepare	guide
prove	behave
escape	frame
dare	dine

Reach Out for New Words

A Write the **ing** form of each new word.

B Each sentence below tells about the actions of a person or animal. Write the **ing** form of the new word that describes these actions.

1. The park ranger is helping the lost campers find their way out of the woods.

    guiding

2. The lion is sneaking out of his cage.

3. Grace is challenging Pam to swim across the lake.

4. The Wilsons are having roast beef, baked potatoes, and a salad.

5. The students are sitting quietly in the classroom.

6. Paula is cutting pieces of wood to fit around her oil painting.

7. Anne is jogging every evening to get ready for the race.

8. The suspect's plane ticket is showing that he was out of town when the store was robbed.

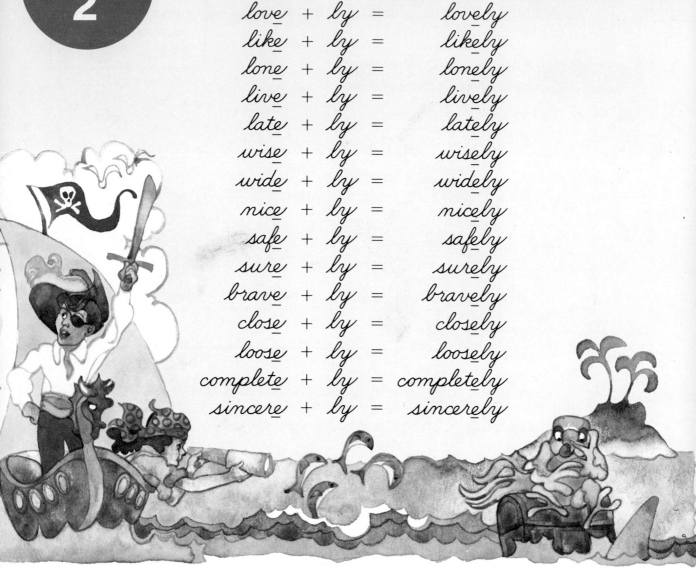

love + ly = lovely
like + ly = likely
lone + ly = lonely
live + ly = lively
late + ly = lately
wise + ly = wisely
wide + ly = widely
nice + ly = nicely
safe + ly = safely
sure + ly = surely
brave + ly = bravely
close + ly = closely
loose + ly = loosely
complete + ly = completely
sincere + ly = sincerely

1. The words in the first column end with what silent letter?
2. What ending was added to make the words in the last column?
3. The letters **a**, **e**, **i**, **o**, and **u** are vowels. The other letters are **consonants**. Does the ending **ly** begin with a consonant or a vowel?
4. Was the **silent e** dropped from each base word before the ending **ly** was added?

When a word ends with **silent e**, do <u>not</u> drop the **e** before you add an ending that begins with a consonant.

Practice the Words

A Use each clue to find a spelling word that fits in the puzzle.

Across

2. nearly
6. a closing for a letter
8. full of energy
10. expected to happen
11. not long ago
12. not tightly

Down

1. over a large area
3. without any doubt
4. in a kind way
5. with courage
7. totally
9. in a smart way

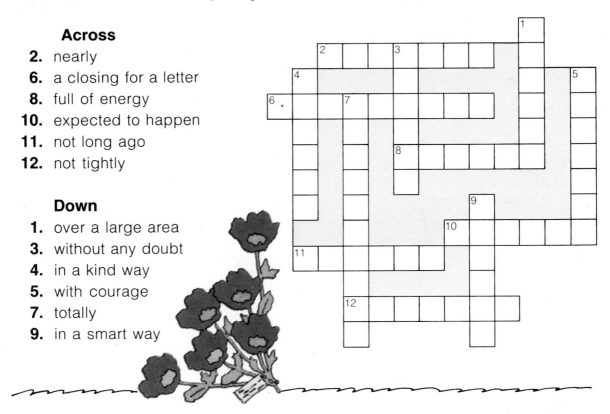

Proofreading

B Read this book report. Five of the underlined words are misspelled. Find the misspelled words. Write them correctly.

The Black Stallion is <u>surely</u> the best book I have ever read. It is about a boy who is lost in a storm at sea. He gets <u>safly</u> to a <u>lovley</u> desert island. It is not <u>likely</u> that anyone will find him. He <u>bravley</u> tries to make the island his home, but he is <u>lonly</u>. Then he meets a beautiful black stallion. They become friends and watch over each other as <u>closely</u> as brothers. The boy becomes <u>completly</u> happy in his island home.

Dictionary

Words in the dictionary are listed in **alphabetical order**. When the first letter of two words is the same, the second letter is used to put them in alphabetical order. Sometimes you will need to use the third, fourth, or another letter to put the words in alphabetical order.

plan

plane

plate

C Write each group of words in alphabetical order.

1. nicely
safely
wisely
bravely
widely
sincerely
surely

2. lively
completely
likely
lonely
loosely
lovely
closely
lately

Build Word Power

Writing

Your spelling words can be used to write about people and the things they do. For example, read the following idea and story.

Idea: a firefighter rescuing people from a burning building

Story: The firefighter *bravely* went into the burning building. It was *likely* that people were inside. They had to be brought out *safely*. He *wisely* put on a mask because the building was *completely* filled with smoke.

Choose one of the story ideas below and write a story using as many spelling words as possible.

a movie star winning an award   a camper seeing a bear
a person stranded on an island   a racer coming in second

lovely	lively	widely	surely	loosely
likely	lately	nicely	bravely	completely
lonely	wisely	safely	closely	sincerely

New Words

strange	separate
secure	immediate
rare	entire

Reach Out for New Words

A Find the **ly** form of a new word that fits in each shape.

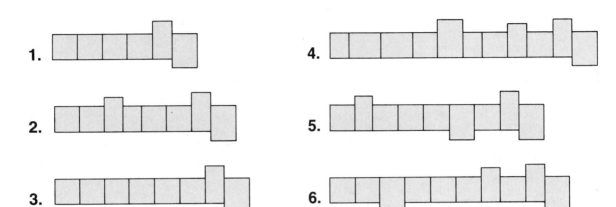

1.
2.
3.
4.
5.
6.

Write the **ly** form of the new word that matches each meaning.

1. totally

2. not together

3. in an unusual way

4. in a safe way

5. not very often

6. right now

Writing

B Use each new **ly** word in a sentence.

15

care + ful = careful
use + ful = useful
hope + ful = hopeful
peace + ful = peaceful
waste + ful = wasteful
grace + ful = graceful
plate + ful = plateful
age + less = ageless
tire + less = tireless
taste + less = tasteless
change + less = changeless
score + less = scoreless
shape + less = shapeless
sleeve + less = sleeveless
home + less = homeless

A **suffix** is an ending added to a word to change the way the word is used.

1. The words in the first column end with what silent letter?
2. What suffix meaning *full of* or *having* has been added to the first seven words?
3. What suffix meaning *without* has been added to the next eight words?
4. Do the suffixes begin with a vowel or a consonant?
5. Was the final **silent e** dropped from each base word when the suffix was added?

When a word ends with **silent e**, do <u>not</u> drop the **e** before you add an ending that begins with a consonant.

A Use each clue to find a spelling word that fits in the boxes. The **silent e** has been given to help you.

1. having a use; helpful

2. forever young

3. does not easily become tired

4. having hope

5. cautious

6. without a place to live

7. not clumsy

8. not at war

9. throws away things that can still be used

10. having no flavor

11. having no shape

12. a 0–0 game

13. always the same

14. without sleeves

B Find the misspelled word in each group. Then write the word correctly.

1. tireless
   changless
   hopeful

2. wakeful
   wasteful
   ageles

3. homeless
   hopeful
   platful

4. tasteless
   carefull
   shapeless

5. usful
   noiseless
   peaceful

6. wasteful
   tireless
   sleevless

17

C Write the spelling word that tells about each person or thing.

1. Bobby threw away a good pair of sneakers because they were dirty. Bobby is ___.

2. That dancer moves well to the music. He is very ___.

3. This meat needs salt and pepper. The meat is ___.

4. Karen thinks her picture may win a prize in the contest. She feels very ___.

5. Jenny has mowed the lawn, trimmed the bushes, and she doesn't need to rest yet. Jenny is ___.

6. This old bathing suit is baggy and loose. It is ___.

7. No one has crossed home plate in the baseball game. The game is ___.

8. There is never any trouble in our town. It is very ___.

9. Lisa ate a big dish of spaghetti and meatballs. She ate a ___.

10. A stray dog is looking for a place to live. He is ___.

Build Word Power

Words that have opposite meanings are called **antonyms.**

Write the spelling word that is the antonym, or opposite, of each word below.

1. thrifty   **3.** old   **5.** warlike   **7.** useless   **9.** hopeless

2. flavorful   **4.** shapely   **6.** reckless   **8.** clumsy   **10.** changing

careful	peaceful	plateful	tasteless	shapeless
useful	wasteful	ageless	changeless	sleeveless
hopeful	graceful	tireless	scoreless	homeless

New Words

price   sense
force   shame
defense   bone

Reach Out for New Words

A Find the **ful** or **less** form of the six new words in this puzzle. Some of the words may overlap. Write each word.

Writing

B Rewrite each sentence to make it more exact. Add the word in parentheses. The first one is done for you.

1. A mother tiger protects her cubs. (defenseless)

A mother tiger protects her defenseless cubs.

2. Fish are easy to eat. (boneless)

3. Ms. Williams kept her jewels in a safe. (priceless)

4. What caused this forest fire? (senseless)

5. The mayor's speech convinced us to clean up the river. (forceful)

6. Bob regretted his actions. (shameful)

Words spelled with ea

dream
speak
meat
cream
least
beneath

head
bread
thread
ahead
meant
weather

break
great
steak

1. What two letters do you see in every word?
2. In how many words do the letters **ea** sound like **ee** in the word **see**?
3. In how many words do the letters **ea** sound like the **e** in the word **ten**?
4. In how many words do the letters **ea** sound like **a** in the word **ape**?

Many words are spelled with the letters **ea.**
The letters **ea** have different sounds.

A Write the spelling words that complete these sentences.

1. I had a ____ and a baked potato for dinner.

2. Today's ____ will be rainy and cool.

3. Use blue ____ to hem your jeans.

4. Potatoes grow ____ the ground.

5. I practice the piano at ____ one hour every day.

6. Dad picked up vegetables, bread, and ____ at the grocery store.

7. Do you ____ when you are sleeping?

8. A police officer will ____ to our class about bicycle safety.

9. This football helmet does not fit my ____ .

10. The baker sold fresh ____ and cakes at the fair.

11. Carol ran ____ of me in the race.

12. I ____ to buy Jim a birthday card, but I forgot.

Proofreading

B Find the eight misspelled words on these signs. Write the words correctly.

On Sale!

Bread	39¢
Meet	$2.29
Cheese	75¢
Round Staek	$1.89
Ice Creme	89¢

Local Bulletins

Local runner sure to braek state record

May 14   Mayor Reed to speek on home safety

May 26   Marvello the Grate to perform at carnival

Detour ahed

Watch Your Hed

C Print the spelling word that fits in the shape and rhymes with the clue word.

1. bake

2. led

3. seem

4. gate

5. feast

6. bed

7. feather

8. teeth

9. team

10. cake

11. fed

12. went

An **analogy** is a special way of showing how words go together. Look at the first pair of words in each row. In what way do these words go together? Write a spelling word that makes the second pair of words go together in the same way as the first pair.

1. **glove** is to **hand**   as   **hat** is to _head_
2. **balloon** is to **pop**   as   **glass** is to ____
3. **beans** is to **vegetable**   as   **pork** is to ____
4. **knit** is to **yarn**   as   **sew** is to ____
5. **hamburger** is to **bun**   as   **jam** is to ____
6. **last** is to **first**   as   **behind** is to ____
7. **dog** is to **bark**   as   **person** is to ____

dream	cream	head	ahead	break
speak	least	bread	meant	great
meat	beneath	thread	weather	steak

New Words

eager	treat
treasure	already
instead	peak
stream	feather

8. **bad** is to **terrible**   as   **good** is to   ____.

9. **biggest** is to **smallest**   as   **most** is to   ____.

10. **cereal** is to **milk**   as   **coffee** is to   ____.

11. **frightening** is to **nightmare**   as   **pleasant** is to   ____.

12. **say** is to **said**   as   **mean** is to   ____.

Reach Out for New Words

A Words are printed in three directions in this puzzle. → ↓ ↘

Find the eight new **ea** words. Write each word. The first letter of each word has been given to help you.

```
c  t  e  a  g  e  r  s
d  b  x  l  z  v  f  t
j  f  k  r  w  b  q  r
s  t  e  e  n  p  m  p
t  r  e  a  s  u  r  e
r  e  g  d  t  l  m  a
e  a  k  y  r  h  q  k
a  t  h  g  j  v  e  s
m  f  l  d  n  h  p  r
c  i  n  s  t  e  a  d
```

1. e____
2. t____
3. i____
4. s____
5. t____
6. a____
7. p____
8. f____

Writing

B Choose five of your new words. On another sheet of paper, write a riddle for each. Give two clues for each riddle. See if a friend can guess the word and write it correctly.

Example: Clue 1: used for sewing

              Clue 2: rhymes with **bread**   *thread*

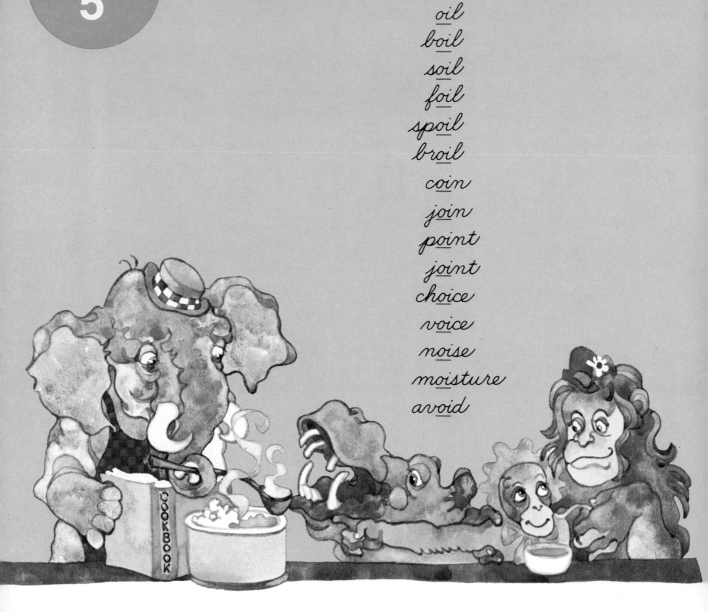

oil
boil
soil
foil
spoil
broil
coin
join
point
joint
choice
voice
noise
moisture
avoid

1. What two letters do you see in every word?
2. Are these letters usually at the beginning,
   in the middle, or at the end of the word?

Many words are spelled with the letters **oi**.
These letters are usually found in the middle of a word.

Practice the Words

Writing

A Write the spelling word that completes each phrase.

1. ___ of a pencil
2. ___ for the garden
3. ___ the water
4. five cent ___
5. a scratching ___
6. ___ our club

7. a sore ___
8. food may ___
9. aluminum ___
10. second ___
11. talk in a low ___
12. grease and ___

Choose four phrases and use each in a sentence.

B Look at each word. If it is spelled correctly, draw a 😊. If it is misspelled, write the correct spelling.

1. koin
2. join
3. voice

4. noice
5. soil
6. briol

7. choise
8. moischure
9. joint

10. foil
11. avoyd
12. point

Dictionary

The two words at the top of each page in the dictionary are called **guide words**. The guide word on the left tells you the first word on the page. The guide word on the right tells you the last word on the page. All the words on the page are listed in alphabetical order between the two guide words.

guide word   guide word

load   mast

load

mast

C The word pairs below are guide words. What spelling words would go on each page? Write them in alphabetical order.

1. **author/crack**

   (5 words)

2. **flower/money**

   (4 words)

3. **night/promise**

   (3 words)

4. **sail/water**

   (3 words)

Build Word Power

Write funny answers for these clues. Write the two rhyming spelling words that go in each pair of blanks.

1. pour water into grease   _spoil_ the _oil_

2. glue two halves of a dime together   ____ the ____

3. tryouts for a glee club   a ____ ____

4. to cook dirt   ____ the ____

5. the sharpest part of your elbow   the ____ of the ____

26

oil	foil	coin	joint	noise
boil	spoil	join	choice	moisture
soil	broil	point	voice	avoid

New Words
Discover new words below!

Reach Out for New Words

A Each number in this code stands for one letter of the alphabet. Decode each word in the paragraphs below. Then write each word.

j	q	f	m	a	i	s	c	g	r	x	b	z	h
1	2	3	4	5	6	7	8	9	10	11	12	13	14

u	p	d	k	o	y	t	e	l	w	v	n
15	16	17	18	19	20	21	22	23	24	25	26

1.   The sailors $\underline{10}$ $\underline{22}$ $\underline{1}$ $\underline{19}$ $\underline{6}$ $\underline{8}$ $\underline{22}$ $\underline{17}$ at the end of a perfect day of sailing. The wind had come up early in the morning. First the sailors had untied the ropes that held the boat. Then they had $\underline{8}$ $\underline{19}$ $\underline{6}$ $\underline{23}$ $\underline{22}$ $\underline{17}$ them on the deck, and $\underline{14}$ $\underline{19}$ $\underline{6}$ $\underline{7}$ $\underline{21}$ $\underline{22}$ $\underline{17}$ the sails. The boat had skimmed across the water all day. Tonight the sky was so clear the sailors thought they could see a planet or an $\underline{5}$ $\underline{7}$ $\underline{21}$ $\underline{22}$ $\underline{10}$ $\underline{19}$ $\underline{6}$ $\underline{17}$ among the stars.

2.   Janet was very $\underline{17}$ $\underline{6}$ $\underline{7}$ $\underline{5}$ $\underline{16}$ $\underline{16}$ $\underline{19}$ $\underline{6}$ $\underline{26}$ $\underline{21}$ $\underline{22}$ $\underline{17}$. A little plant had spoiled her vacation. She hadn't known that the three-leaved vine was $\underline{16}$ $\underline{19}$ $\underline{6}$ $\underline{7}$ $\underline{19}$ $\underline{26}$ ivy! Now, instead of going swimming she had an $\underline{5}$ $\underline{16}$ $\underline{16}$ $\underline{19}$ $\underline{6}$ $\underline{26}$ $\underline{21}$ $\underline{4}$ $\underline{22}$ $\underline{26}$ $\underline{21}$ with the doctor!

B Write the new **oi** word that fits each meaning.

1. a tiny planet
2. a planned meeting
3. something harmful
4. lifted up
5. was very happy
6. wound in circles

they	+ will	=	they'll
they	+ are	=	they're
here	+ is	=	here's
she	+ is	=	she's
there	+ is	=	there's
you	+ would	=	you'd
they	+ would	=	they'd
we	+ would	=	we'd
does	+ not	=	doesn't
would	+ not	=	wouldn't
will	+ not	=	won't
has	+ not	=	hasn't
have	+ not	=	haven't
could	+ not	=	couldn't
should	+ not	=	shouldn't

1. The words in the last column are **contractions**. Each contraction is made from how many words?
2. Were any letters left out when the words were joined?
3. In each contraction an **apostrophe** takes the place of one or more letters. Write an apostrophe.

A contraction is made from two words. When the two words are joined, an **apostrophe** (') takes the place of one or more letters. The contraction **won't** is special. When the words **will** and **not** are put together, changes are made in both words.

will + not = won't

28

A Copy the chart on your paper. Write the contractions in alphabetical order in the first column. Then answer the questions to complete the chart.

	Contraction	What two words does it stand for?	What letter(s) does the apostrophe (') replace?
1.	couldn't	could not	o
2.			
3.			
4.			
5.			
6.			
7.			
8.			
9.			
10.		they will	
11.			
12.			
13.			(also change **will** to **wo**)
14.			
15.			

B Write the contraction for each pair of words. Each contraction should fit in the boxes. An apostrophe fills one box.

1. should not
2. there is
3. they are
4. we would
5. has not

29

C Find each pair of words that can be made into a contraction. Then write the contractions.

1. Here is the shoe I could not find yesterday.

2. They will have a cookout on Sunday if it does not rain.

3. Sara will not bake a cake if you would prefer cookies.

4. My parents have not found a house they would like to buy.

5. It would not surprise me if Joan has not been told.

Build Word Power

Complete this word chain using the words shown below. Begin by finding the word that ends with the letter **l** and fits in the seven spaces in that row. Count one space for the apostrophe.

they'd
they'll
won't
doesn't
hasn't
haven't
we'd
you'd

On another sheet of paper, try to make your own word chain.

they'll	she's	they'd	wouldn't	haven't
they're	there's	we'd	won't	couldn't
here's	you'd	doesn't	hasn't	shouldn't

Reach Out for New Words

A The words that form each new contraction fit in the sets of lines and letters. The contractions fit in the boxes. Write the words and contraction that go with each set of lines and boxes. Remember to count one box for the apostrophe.

1. _ _ _ _n_ _ _ _

2. _ _ _ _ _ _ _i_ _

3. _ _ _ _ _ _o_ _

4. _ _ _ _ _ h a _ _ _

5. _ _ w i _ _ _

6. _ h _ _ _ _ _ _ _

7. _ f _ t h e _ _ _ _ _ _

	w	h	e	n	'	s	
1							
2							
3							
4							
5							
6							
7							

B Rewrite each sentence. Replace the underlined words with a contraction.

1. <u>They have</u> already finished the game.

2. Joe <u>must not</u> tell his sister about the surprise party.

3. I think <u>it will</u> reach ninety degrees today.

4. Sam will meet you at four <u>of the clock</u>.

5. <u>Who will</u> win the five-mile race?

Words spelled with ie or ei

chief
niece
piece
field
fierce
shield
brief
believe
cashier

receive
ceiling

eight
weigh
neighbor
reindeer

1. The letters **i** and **e** are in each of these words.
   In how many words do you see the letters **ie**?
   In how many words do you see the letters **ei**?
2. Look at the words **receive** and **ceiling**.
   Do you see the letters **ei** or **ie** after the letter **c**?
3. Find the four words in which you hear the
   sound of the letter **a**. Do you see **ei** or **ie**?

This rhyme will help you spell words that have the letters **i** and **e**.

i before e
except after c
or when sounded like a
as in neighbor or weigh

32

Practice the Words

A Write the spelling words that complete these sentences.

1. The ____ gave me 59¢ in change.
2. The baseball game was postponed because of a muddy ____ .
3. There is a ____ missing from this jigsaw puzzle.
4. I like to ____ mail from my pen pal.
5. The ____ of police spoke to the other officers.
6. The grocer will ____ those apples on the scale.
7. Mrs. Yoshi took her ____ and nephew to the zoo.
8. I will need a ladder when I paint the ____ .
9. The score of the baseball game was ____ to five.
10. The ____ news report lasted only thirty seconds.
11. A ____ thunderstorm blew over a tree in our yard.
12. The knight wore a suit of armor and carried a ____ .

B Print the spelling word that fits in each shape.

1.

2.

3.

4.

5.

6.

7.

8.

9.

10.

11.

12.

33

Dictionary

The words listed on a dictionary page are called **entry words.**
They are printed in dark letters to help you find them.

Entry words are divided into word parts called **syllables.**
A dot or space shows where a word is divided into syllables.

an·gry (ang′grē) *adj.* feeling or showing
anger. **an′ gri·er, an′ gri·est —an′gri·ly**
adv.

How many syllables
are in the word **angry**? _____

C Write the words below in alphabetical order. Look up each word in your
dictionary. Then write the word again, putting a dot between the syllables.

believe   reindeer   neighbor   ceiling   receive   cashier

Build Word Power

Unscramble each group of letters to make the spelling words that fit in the
boxes.

1. c e e r i f
2. g l i n i c e
3. c e e n i
4. v e e r i c e
5. s h a c i r e
6. l e b e v i e
7. l e f i d
8. f e c h i
9. g i w e h
10. b o r e i g h n

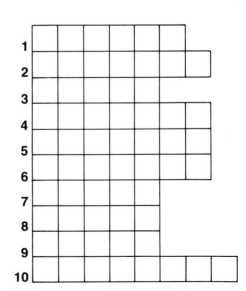

34

chief	field	brief	receive	weigh
niece	fierce	believe	ceiling	neighbor
piece	shield	cashier	eight	reindeer

New Words

retrieve	sleigh
conceited	relief
frontier	freight
weight	yield

Reach Out for New Words

A You learned a rhyme on page 32 that helps you remember how to spell many **ie** and **ei** words. Write the new words that go with each part of the rhyme.

> **i** before **e** (4 words)
>
> except after **c** (1 word)
>
> or when sounded like **a** (2 words)
>
> as in **neighbor** or **weigh** (1 word)

Writing

B Write a new **ei** or **ie** word that has almost the same meaning as each word or phrase below.

1. bring back

2. ounces

3. sled

4. cargo

5. unexplored land

6. give way to

7. pain becoming less

8. too proud

Write one sentence using two of the new **ie** words. Write another sentence using two new **ei** words.

1
invite inviting
surprise surprising
promise promising

2
love lovely
complete completely
sincere sincerely

3
care careful
hope hopeful
sleeve sleeveless

4
speak
bread
break

5
coin
join
choice

6
they'll
doesn't
won't

7
believe
receive
neighbor

Using Review Words

A An analogy is a special way of showing how words go together. Look at the first pair of words in each row. In what way do these words go together? Write a spelling word that makes the second pair of words go together in the same way as the first pair.

1. **love** is to **lovely**   as   **sincere** is to ____

2. **receive** is to **receiving**   as   **promise** is to ____

3. **would not** is to **wouldn't**   as   **does not** is to ____

4. **sincerely** is to **sincere**   as   **completely** is to ____

5. **believe** is to **believing**   as   **invite** is to ____

6. **careless** is to **careful**   as   **hopeless** is to ____

7. **you would** is to **you'd**   as   **will not** is to ____

8. **promising** is to **promise**   as   **surprising** is to ____

9. **hope** is to **hopeless**   as   **sleeve** is to ____

Proofreading

B Find each misspelled word. Write the correct spelling.

1. It is serprising that the vase didn't braek.

2. We invited our nieghbor to have dinner with us.

3. I'm hopefull that I'll recieve a good grade on that paper.

4. Do you sincerly beleive what you just said?

5. Craig may have the first choise.

6. They'l be carefull not to touch the wet paint.

C Write the word from the box that goes in each blank.

> bread believe coin receive speak neighbor
> break choice they'll lovely join completely

1. a ten cent ____

2. ____ the window

3. ____ finished

4. ____ the club

5. I think ____ agree

6. a slice of ____

7. our next door ____

8. ____ in ghosts

9. a ____ dress

10. ____ another language

11. ____ a letter

12. first ____

Using More Review Words

A Use the directions following each base word to make another form of the word.

1. we   form a contraction with **would**

2. peace   write the **ful** form

3. there   form a contraction with **is**

4. tire   write the **less** form

5. slide   write the **ing** form

6. lone   write the **ly** form

7. serve   write the **ing** form

8. sure   write the **ly** form

9. fierce   write the **ly** form

10. you   form a contraction with **would**

11. wise   write the **ly** form

12. use   write the **ful** form

13. lose   write the **ing** form

14. shape   write the **less** form

B Three words in each row follow the same spelling pattern. One word does not. Find that word. Be ready to tell why it does not belong.

1. boil meat soil joint
   (**Meat** is the only word spelled with **ea**.)
2. cashier reindeer field piece
3. hasn't haven't wouldn't they're
4. nicely bravely scoring closely
5. boiling sharing voting shining
6. least cream meat refuse
7. neighbor eight chief weigh
8. spoiling dreaming sharing pointing
9. here's they'd she's there's
10. trading wasteful ageless likely

C An analogy is a special way of showing how words go together. Look at the first pair of words in each row. In what way do these words go together? Write a word from the box that makes the second pair of words go together in the same way as the first pair.

ceiling	head	niece	bouncing	refusing
thread	fierce	eight	weigh	shining

1. **knit** is to **yarn** as **sew** is to _____
2. **shoe** is to **foot** as **hat** is to _____
3. **below** is to **floor** as **above** is to _____
4. **yes** is to **accepting** as **no** is to _____
5. **inches** are to **measure** as **pounds** are to _____
6. **lamb** is to **timid** as **lion** is to _____
7. **star** is to **twinkling** as **sun** is to _____
8. **four** is to **five** as **seven** is to _____
9. **football** is to **kicking** as **basketball** is to _____
10. **brother** is to **sister** as **nephew** is to _____

forward	breathing	soccer	bandaged
screaming	banner	skinned	soreness
bleachers	backward	goal	bleeding
shooting	court	wildly	moment
barely	toward	lying	limped

Prewriting. Prewriting is the thinking and planning you do before you begin to write. In this lesson, you will plan and write a **paragraph that tells what happened.**

Use Prewriting Skills

A Get ready to write about what happened at a sports event. You might choose a soccer game or basketball game, for example. Answer these questions with spelling words. The words will help you think of ideas for your paragraph.

1. What word names a sport?

2. What words tell the direction a player is moving? (3 words)

3. What **ed** action verbs could you use in your paragraph? (3 words)

4. What **ing** verbs might describe actions at a sports event? (5 words)

5. Where might the fans sit? What might they wave?

6. On what is a basketball game played? What does the player score?

7. What **ly** words could describe a player's actions? (2 words)

B To plan a paragraph well, make notes about your topic. Write down your ideas. You will notice that many of your notes will tell about one particular idea. This can be the **main idea** of your paragraph.

Here are some prewriting notes Jody wrote about her first soccer game.

flat tire on the way	limped off the field
barely on time for the game	coach bandaged my leg
fell backward and skinned my knee	soccer is good exercise
my brother plays basketball	soreness lasted long after the game

Jody looked over her notes. Here's what she decided her main idea should be:

Everything went wrong the day I played my first soccer game.

Not all of Jody's notes fit that idea. Find those that do not belong. Then write the notes that do tell about Jody's main idea.

C The ideas in a paragraph must be in an order that makes sense. When you write a paragraph that tells a story, put the ideas in the order that they happened.

Look at the prewriting notes you wrote for Exercise B. Number them in an order that makes sense.

Now Think

Plan your own paragraph about a sports event. Think about games you have seen or played. How did the fans act? What did the players do? Which moments were most exciting? You can make up your story or tell about something that really happened.

Follow these prewriting steps:

1. Choose your topic.
2. Make a list of ideas about your topic.
3. Read your notes to see how they fit together.
4. Decide on a main idea about your topic.
5. Cross out ideas that don't belong.
6. Number the rest in an order that makes sense.

Writing. Begin your paragraph with a topic sentence that tells the main idea. Write other sentences that tell about what happened. These sentences should add details about your main idea.

Use Writing Skills

Use good details to make your writing interesting. Expand each sentence by adding details to the simple subject and verb.

Example: Simple Subject → The <u>coach</u> | <u>shouted</u> . ← **Verb**

The excited soccer <u>coach</u> wildly <u>shouted</u> advice to the team captain.

1. <u>Fans</u> <u>were screaming</u>.

2. The <u>soreness</u> <u>lasted</u>.

3. The <u>bleachers</u> <u>were filled</u>.

4. The <u>banner</u> <u>is hanging</u>.

5. The <u>moment</u> <u>had arrived</u>.

6. <u>Lauren</u> <u>limped</u>.

7. <u>Doug</u> <u>was shooting</u>.

Now Write   Look at your prewriting notes. Use them to write a paragraph about a sports event. Begin with a strong topic sentence that tells what the paragraph is about. Tell things in the order that they happened. Try to write interesting sentences that have good details.

Revising and Proofreading. Your writing is not finished until you have revised your paragraph. When you revise, you make changes to improve your writing. First revise your ideas. Change words or sentences to make them better. Then proofread carefully to find mistakes in capitalization, punctuation, and spelling.

One important part of revising is checking to see that you have chosen lively language. In a paragraph that tells what happened, you want to use verbs that show vivid action.

> **Example:** Chris <u>went</u> to first base. (weak verb)
> Chris <u>raced</u> to first base. (strong verb)

Use Revising and Proofreading Skills

A Rewrite the following sentences. Replace the underlined words with spelling words. The spelling words should be verbs that show vivid action.

1. The fans were <u>making noise</u> in the stands.

2. One player was <u>throwing</u> the ball at the basket.

3. Suddenly she tripped and <u>hurt</u> her knee.

4. The injured player <u>walked</u> off the court.

B Proofread this first part of a paragraph about a baseball game. Find the mistakes in capitalization, punctuation, and spelling. Then rewrite the paragraph correctly on your own paper.

Remember
- Begin every sentence with a capital letter.
- Indent the first line of a paragraph.
- End every sentence with the correct end mark.

My gaol in baseball was to reach first base. the coach sent me to bat in every game I struck out wildly every time At last my momeant came? I was breething hard as I waited for the pitch. Would I finally get my single.

C Revise the following paragraph. Then rewrite it correctly on your own paper. The directions below will help you.

1. Find one sentence that is not about the main idea.
2. Find one sentence that is out of order.
3. Replace the two underlined verbs with stronger verbs from your spelling list.
4. Find the six misspelled words. Write them correctly.
5. Correct the capitalization errors in lines 3 and 8.
6. Correct one punctuation error in line 4.

1   Wilson Clark was the hero of the Hilltop basketball team yesterday.

2   Hilltop had won by two points! The score was tied a moment before the

3 game ended. A forwerd quickly passed the ball to wilson. He raced all

4 the way down the cort and suddenly fell backward He landed on his

5 back, but he was still holding the ball. He knew he didn't have time to get

6 up and continue running. There wasn't even time to pass the ball to

7 another player. Wilson realized that there was only one thing to do.

8 Lyeng on the floor, he tried <u>throwing</u> a basket. he scord the goal as the

9 buzzer ended the game. Fans in the bleechers began <u>calling</u> wildley the

10 minute the buzzer sounded. Wilson gets good grades too.

Now Revise

Read your own sports story. Does each sentence tell about the main idea? Are your sentences in an order that makes sense? Have you used the best words? Remember to proofread for mistakes in capitalization, punctuation, and spelling. Copy the paragraph in your best handwriting.

Now you've written a paragraph you should be proud of. Share your paragraph with other students. Show them how you are learning the process of writing.

A Writer's Journal

Reading poetry can give you ideas for writing in your journal. A poem may talk about feelings or experiences you have had. A poem may also help you see ordinary things in fresh, new ways.

SINCE HANNA MOVED AWAY

The tires on my bike are flat.
The sky is grouchy gray.
At least it sure feels like that
Since Hanna moved away.

Chocolate ice cream tastes
    like prunes.
December's come to stay.
They've taken back the Mays
    and Junes
Since Hanna moved away.

Flowers smell like halibut.
Velvet feels like hay.
Every handsome dog's a mutt
Since Hanna moved away.

Nothing's fun to laugh about.
Nothing's fun to play.
They call me, but I won't
    come out
Since Hanna moved away.

—JUDITH VIORST

Read the poem and think about what it means. Then discuss the questions with the class.

1. Who is Hanna? How does the speaker feel about Hanna?

2. What does the speaker mean by lines such as "Chocolate ice cream tastes like prunes" or "Velvet feels like hay"? What do these things have to do with a friend moving away?

Now use the poem as a starting point for your next journal entry. Here are some ideas you might want to use:

1. Write about a friend who moved away. Describe how you felt.

2. The speaker in the poem describes her feelings by telling us that many good things no longer seem good. Write about an experience that made you sad or angry. You may want to describe your feelings the way the speaker in the poem describes hers. Use the following as sentence ideas:

_____ tasted like _____.
_____ smelled like _____.

Building a Personal Word List

If you do not know how to spell a word, follow these steps.
1. Write the word as you think it should be spelled.
2. After writing, see if the word is on your personal word list. If not, look up the word in the dictionary.
3. Correct your spelling. Add the word to your personal word list.
4. Practice spelling the word several times.

Lesson 10

Plurals of final y words

holiday	holidays
highway	highways
chimney	chimneys
jockey	jockeys
journey	journeys
subway	subways
display	displays
story	stories
country	countries
family	families
canary	canaries
duty	duties
library	libraries
blueberry	blueberries
flurry	flurries

A word that names something is called a **noun**.
A noun that names *one* thing is a **singular** noun.
A noun that names *more than one* thing is a **plural** noun.

1. The words in the first column are singular. How many end with **vowel + y**?
   How many end with **consonant + y**?
2. The words in the second column are plural.
   What is the last letter of the **vowel + y** words?
   What are the last three letters of the **consonant + y** words?

To make the plural form of a noun that ends with **vowel + y**,
   add the letter **s**.
To make the plural form of a noun that ends with **consonant + y**,
   change the **y** to **i** and add **es**.

Practice the Words

A Print the spelling word that fits in each shape.

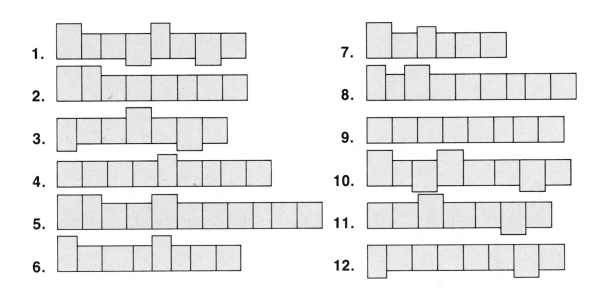

1.

2.

3.

4.

5.

6.

7.

8.

9.

10.

11.

12.

B Write the seven base words that go in the blanks.
Then write the plural form of each word.

Last fall, my **1** decided to spend the Labor
Day **2** in the **3**. As we drove down the **4**, we
each took turns telling a **5**, and then we all
sang songs. After a time, we drove through a
beautiful valley. It was filled with apple
trees, **6** bushes, and fields of vegetables.
There was only one house in the valley. It was
very large and had a tall **7**. My little brother
wondered if a green giant lived there.

47

C Use the clues to find the spelling words that fit in the puzzle.

Across

2. yellow birds
5. special days
6. jobs
10. underground trains
11. places where books are kept
12. people who ride horses

Down

1. brothers, sisters, and parents
3. fairy tales
4. smoke goes up these
7. trips
8. shows
9. a few snowflakes

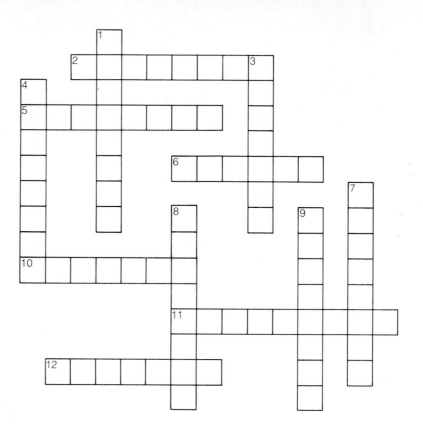

Build Word Power

Each word below is part of a plural spelling word. Write the spelling word. Use each word only once.

1. key   **3.** high   **5.** am   **7.** our   **9.** or   **11.** is

2. can   **4.** lid   **6.** ties   **8.** him   **10.** tries   **12.** blue

holidays   jockeys   displays   families   libraries
highways   journeys   stories   canaries   blueberries
chimneys   subways   countries   duties   flurries

New Words
Discover new words below!

Reach Out for New Words

A Use the code to find seven new words that are described by the sentences. Each number stands for one letter of the alphabet. Write the words.

j	q	f	m	a	i	s	c	g	r	x	b	z	h
1	2	3	4	5	6	7	8	9	10	11	12	13	14

u	p	d	k	o	y	t	e	l	w	v	n
15	16	17	18	19	20	21	22	23	24	25	26

1. Football players wear them. 1 22 10 7 22 20 7

2. Machines are used to make things here. 3 5 8 21 19 10 6 22 7

3. You shop for these in the supermarket. 9 10 19 8 22 10 6 22 7

4. They make a flashlight shine. 12 5 21 21 22 10 6 22 7

5. Winners often receive them. 21 10 19 16 14 6 22 7

6. Trains run on them. 10 5 6 23 24 5 20 7

7. Pads and helmets protect athletes from them. 6 26 1 15 10 6 22 7

Dictionary

B Write the new words in alphabetical order. Then write the base form of each word. Look up each base word in your spelling dictionary. Write the base word again, putting dots between the syllables.

Spelling Words	Base Words	Syllables

Lesson 11

Consonant + y words with the endings er and est

tiny	tinier	tiniest
busy	busier	busiest
early	earlier	earliest
icy	icier	iciest
curly	curlier	curliest
angry	angrier	angriest
friendly	friendlier	friendliest
silly	sillier	silliest

A word that describes a noun is called an **adjective**.

1. What is the last letter of each word in the first column?
2. Is the letter before the **y** a vowel or a consonant?
3. What are the last two letters of the words in the second column?
4. What are the last three letters of the words in the third column?
5. When **er** and **est** were added to the words in the first column, the final **y** was changed to what letter?

The ending **er** can be added to make an adjective mean *more*.
    Spot is tinier than Pepper.
The ending **est** can be added to make an adjective mean *most*.
    Spot is the tiniest of the three dogs.
When an adjective ends with **consonant + y**, change the **y** to **i** before you add **er** or **est**.

50

A Write the form of the spelling word in parentheses that goes in each blank. Use the **er** form when you compare two people or things. Use the **est** form when you compare three or more people or things.

1. The sidewalk is ____ than the driveway. (icy)

2. Tom is the ____ boy in our class. (friendly)

3. The sun sets ____ in the winter than in summer. (early)

4. That joke is even ____ than the one Janet told. (silly)

5. The ____ puppy in the litter is the one I want. (tiny)

6. On what day of the year is the ____ sunrise? (early)

7. My sister has the ____ hair in our family. (curly)

8. The ____ clown in the circus wears a bright orange wig. (silly)

9. Monday is the ____ day of the week for me. (busy)

10. That newborn hamster is ____ than a quarter. (tiny)

11. A poodle has _____ hair than a collie. (curly)

12. The fans were _____ than the losing team. (angry)

B Find the misspelled word in each group. Write the word correctly.

1. erlier
   curly
   busiest
   tiniest

2. curlier
   friendlyer
   busy
   earliest

3. friendliest
   curly
   silliest
   angryest

4. early
   angry
   sillier
   curlliest

5. tinier
   silly
   busyer
   icy

6. friendly
   angrier
   tiny
   iceyest

51

C Unscramble the **er** form of each spelling word and write it. Then write the **est** form.

1. larriee

2. brusie

3. riniet

4. slirile

5. rangeir

6. drieflienr

7. ricie

8. licreur

Build Word Power

Writing

Each sentence below gives you some information. Write a question you might ask to find out more information. Use the **er** or **est** form of a spelling word in your question.

1. Betty and Meg have <u>curly</u> hair.

   Whose hair is curlier?

2. All the students in our class are <u>friendly</u>.

3. The clowns in this circus are <u>silly</u>.

4. Barb and Suzanne have <u>tiny</u> dogs.

5. Monday and Tuesday will be very <u>busy</u> days.

tinier	busiest	icier	curliest	friendlier	silliest
tiniest	earlier	iciest	angrier	friendliest	
busier	earliest	curlier	angriest	sillier	

New Words

merry	dizzy
fancy	hazy
greedy	juicy
ugly	

Reach Out for New Words

A Write the **er** and **est** forms of each new word.

B Write the **est** form of the new word that describes each person or thing below.

1. the dress with the most
   lace and ribbons on it   the ____ dress

2. the mask with green skin,
   bloodshot eyes, and a wart   the ____ mask

3. the orange with the most
   liquid inside it   the ____ orange

4. the room with the most dust
   and smoke in it   the ____ room

5. the boy who turned the most
   cartwheels   the ____ boy

6. the puppy who ate the whole
   box of dog biscuits   the ____ puppy

7. the party at which everyone
   had a wonderful time   the ____ party

try	*trying*	*tried*
deny	*denying*	*denied*
reply	*replying*	*replied*
bury	*burying*	*buried*
study	*studying*	*studied*
worry	*worrying*	*worried*
empty	*emptying*	*emptied*
multiply	*multiplying*	*multiplied*

A **verb** is a word that tells about an action.
A verb that tells about an action that happened in the past is in
the **past tense**.

1. The words in the first column can all be verbs.
   Is the letter before each final **y** a consonant or a vowel?
2. What three letters were added to make the words in the second column?
3. Did the **y** change before **ing** was added?
4. The words in the last column are in the past tense.
   What are the last two letters of these words?
5. What happened to the **y** when the **ed** was added?

When an ending is added to a verb that ends with **consonant + y**,
change the **y** to **i** unless the ending is **ing**.

Practice the Words

A Complete each sentence with the **ed** or **ing** form of a spelling word.

1. The pirate _____ the treasure near a large rock.

2. Kay didn't sleep because she was _____ about her grades.

3. Lou is _____ the wastebaskets.

4. I was still _____ when the math test ended.

5. The swimmer _____ to beat the school record.

6. Pat is _____ to the letter from his pen pal.

7. Alex is _____ for the history test.

8. Mom _____ the carton of milk into the pitcher.

9. I got the right answer when I _____ the two numbers.

10. Tom is _____ to fix the chain on his bike.

11. Chris _____ correctly to the teacher's question.

12. Ben _____ hard for the science test.

13. Our dog is _____ his bone in the backyard.

14. Barry _____ having started the rumor.

15. The farmer _____ about the crops when it got cold.

B Look at each word. If it is spelled correctly, draw a 😊. If it is misspelled, write the word correctly.

1. bureying
2. spying
3. marrying
4. repliing
5. multiplyed
6. tryed
7. empteing
8. worying
9. crying
10. denyed
11. copied
12. studyed

Dictionary

A dictionary **entry** is made up of an **entry word** and all the information that follows it.

Many entry words are base words. Words with endings, or **word forms**, are often included in the entries for base words.

> **try** (trī) *v.* to make an effort.
> —**tried, try′ ing**

For example, the word forms **tried** and **trying** are included in the entry for **try**.

C What entry word would you look up to find each word?

1. trying

2. multiplying

3. replied

4. worried

5. buried

6. emptied

7. studying

8. denying

Build Word Power

Writing

Write a sentence to answer each question. Use the past tense of the underlined word.

1. How long did you <u>study</u> last night?

2. What numbers did you <u>multiply</u>?

3. Where did the dog <u>bury</u> the bone?

4. What did you <u>try</u> to make?

5. What did the coach <u>worry</u> about?

6. What did he <u>deny</u> having done?

trying	denied	burying	studied	emptying	multiplied
tried	replying	buried	worrying	emptied	
denying	replied	studying	worried	multiplying	

New Word

magnify
pity
occupy
supply
steady
satisfy

Reach Out for New Words

A Write the **ing** form and the past tense of each new word.

B Use each clue to find a new word that fits in the puzzle. Each word will end with **ed** or **ing**.

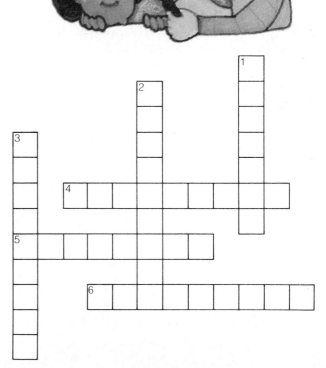

Across

4. providing things
5. kept from moving
6. made something look larger

Down

1. feeling sorry for
2. living in
3. pleased

paw   drawing
law   crawling
claw   yawned
straw   thawed
lawn   sawdust
dawn   outlaw
shawl   coleslaw
           strawberry

Look at the first seven words.

1. What two letters do you see in every word?
2. How many syllables are in each word?
3. In how many words does **aw** come at the end?
4. In how many words is **aw** followed by **n**?
5. In how many words is **aw** followed by **l**?

Look at the next eight words.

6. How many words have the ending **ing**?   **ed**?

> The letters **aw** are found in many one-syllable words.
> They may come at the end of the word or just before **l** or **n** .

58

A Use each clue to find a spelling word that fits in the boxes. The letter **a** has been given to help you.

1. a dog's foot

2. short grass around a house

3. when the sun comes up

4. opened your mouth sleepily

5. wood dust left after sawing

6. a sharp nail on an animal's foot

7. clothing that wraps around the shoulders

8. became unfrozen

9. making a picture

10. moving on hands and knees

11. a tube for drinking

12. a red fruit

13. someone who breaks laws

14. a cabbage salad

Words that have almost the same meaning are called **synonyms.**

B Write the spelling word that is the synonym of each word below.

1. melted   3. sunrise   5. foot   7. hay

2. rule   4. sketching   6. nail   8. creeping

C Unscramble each group of letters to make a spelling word.

1. nawl
2. clingwar
3. wap
4. warst
5. awl
6. wringad
7. dawney
8. whated
9. tusswad
10. twalou
11. lawc
12. brewstarry
13. washl
14. dwan
15. scloawle

Build Word Power

Write the spelling word that goes with each word group.

1. orange, cherry, apple, ____
2. hopping, creeping, walking, ____
3. painting, sketching, coloring, ____
4. cape, sweater, jacket, ____
5. afternoon, evening, noon, ____
6. foot, hoof, hand, ____
7. French fries, baked beans, potato salad, ____
8. whistled, chewed, talked, ____

paw	straw	shawl	yawned	outlaw
law	lawn	drawing	thawed	coleslaw
claw	dawn	crawling	sawdust	strawberry

Reach Out for New Words

A Words are printed in three directions in this puzzle. → ↓ ↘ Find the nine new **aw** words. Write each word on your paper.

```
j r h f l a w s d
k p a a c b g p f
q l a w y e r r b
s m n n h l r a a
x c w v t i s w w
v d r c b f d l l
k g p a d z v e i
s c r a w l e d n
h t l a w n i n g
n m s c b q y w j
```

Writing

B Write four sentences using two or more **aw** words in each sentence. Use all your new **aw** words. You may also use list words. Circle the **aw** words in each sentence.

I yawned when I woke at dawn to mow the lawn.

fault
haunt
launch
laundry
faucet
August
author
autumn
sauce
saucer
because
applaud
caught
taught
daughter

1. What two letters do you see in every word?
2. Do these letters come at the end of the word?

The letters **au** are usually found at the beginning or in the middle of a word.

A Use each clue to find a spelling word that fits in the puzzle.

Across

3. gravy
6. to clap hands
7. to set off a rocket
8. a dish under a cup
11. helped someone learn
13. a female child
14. what a ghost does

Down

1. for this reason
2. blame
4. the month after July
5. what water comes through
7. clothes to be washed
9. a writer
10. captured
12. the season after summer

B Answer each question with spelling words.

1. Which three words begin with the letters **au**?

2. Which three words have the letters **augh**?

3. Which three words have the letters **aun**?

4. Which three words have the letters **auce**?

Proofreading

C Find the eight misspelled words in the newspaper advertisements and headlines below. Write each word correctly.

Critics Aplaud Play by Local Auther

SQUEAKY CLEANERS

- Complete lawndry service available
- We remove all stains, from grass to spaghetti sauce

576 Main Street

Leaky faucet?
Call Pete the Plumber!
555-8247

Rain at Fawlt in Delayed Rocket Launch

Schools Close Becuse of Snow

Millers' Department Store
AUTUM CHINA SALE!
Buy a dinner plate, cup and sauser for $15!
Service for 8 only $110!
No payments until Augist!

Build Word Power

One word will sometimes make you think of another word. For example, the word **paw** may make you think of a <u>dog</u> because a dog's foot is called a paw.

Each underlined word below goes with one of your spelling words. Write the spelling word. Then write a sentence using both words.

1. <u>Ghost</u> goes with ____ .

4. <u>Ball</u> goes with ____ .

2. <u>Cup</u> goes with ____ .

5. <u>Water</u> goes with ____ .

3. <u>Story</u> goes with ____ .

fault	laundry	author	saucer	caught
haunt	faucet	autumn	because	taught
launch	August	sauce	applaud	daughter

New Words
Discover new words below!

Reach Out for New Words

A Find eight new **au** words by following this code. Each letter in a word goes with a capital letter and a number. For example: B2 = h.

	A	B	C	D
1	g	u	s	p
2	a	h	t	e
3	o	c	r	u
4	i	y	d	f
5	b	m	n	l

1. <u>A2</u> <u>D3</u> <u>C2</u> <u>A3</u> <u>B5</u> <u>A2</u> <u>C2</u> <u>A4</u> <u>B3</u>

2. <u>A2</u> <u>D3</u> <u>C4</u> <u>A4</u> <u>C2</u> <u>A3</u> <u>C3</u> <u>A4</u> <u>D3</u> <u>B5</u>

3. <u>C1</u> <u>A2</u> <u>D3</u> <u>C1</u> <u>A2</u> <u>A1</u> <u>D2</u>

4. <u>A2</u> <u>D3</u> <u>C2</u> <u>A3</u> <u>B5</u> <u>A3</u> <u>A5</u> <u>A4</u> <u>D5</u> <u>D2</u>

5. <u>D1</u> <u>A2</u> <u>D3</u> <u>C1</u> <u>D2</u>

6. <u>A2</u> <u>D3</u> <u>C4</u> <u>A4</u> <u>D2</u> <u>C5</u> <u>B3</u> <u>D2</u>

7. <u>A2</u> <u>D3</u> <u>B3</u> <u>C2</u> <u>A4</u> <u>A3</u> <u>C5</u>

8. <u>C5</u> <u>A2</u> <u>D3</u> <u>A1</u> <u>B2</u> <u>C2</u> <u>B4</u>

B Add the missing vowels to complete each word. Then match each word with its meaning.

1. _ _ d _ _ nc _   behaving badly
2. p _ _ s _   a special kind of sale
3. n _ _ ghty   a kind of breakfast meat
4. _ _ t _ m _ b _ l _   people seeing a play or concert
5. _ _ d _ t _ r _ _ m   a short stop
6. _ _ ct _ _ n   keeps working by itself
7. _ _ t _ m _ t _ c   a car
8. s _ _ s _ g _   a large room for performances

65

shout   eyebrow
proud   clown
sour   drown
blouse   howl
ounce   growl
pound   flower
thousand   power
amount

1. In how many words do you see the letters **ou**?
2. Does **ou** ever come at the end of a word?
   at the beginning? in the middle?
3. In how many words do you see the letters **ow**?
4. Does **ow** ever come at the end of a word?
5. What letter or letters come after **ow** in **clown** and **drown**?
   in **howl** and **growl**? in **flower** and **power**?

Sometimes it is difficult to decide whether to spell a word with the letters
   ou or **ow**.
The letters **ou** are usually found at the beginning or in the middle of a word.
The letters **ow** are usually found at the end of a word or followed by one **n**,
   one **l**, or the letters **er**.

Practice the Words

A Use each clue to find a spelling word that fits in the boxes.

1. yell

2. the cry of a wolf

3. snarl

4. a shirt

5. opposite of **sweet**

6. how much

7. sixteen of these make a pound

8. pleased with yourself

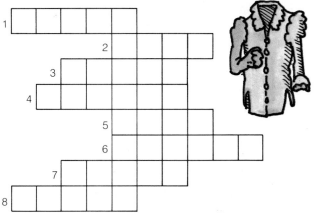

9. a measure of weight

10. hair above the eye

11. a rose

12. strength

13. a funny person

B Look at each word. If it is spelled correctly, draw a ☺. If it is misspelled, write the word correctly.

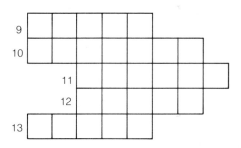

1. sour

2. power

3. thousend

4. showt

5. proud

6. growel

7. flower

8. amownt

9. drown

10. cloun

11. bloues

12. ownse

Dictionary

C The words below are dictionary guide words. What spelling words would appear on the same page as each pair of guide words? Write them in alphabetical order.

1. shore/town

(3 words)

2. cheese/eyelash

(3 words)

3. flat/huddle

(3 words)

4. other/puddle

(4 words)

5. among/cabin

(2 words)

Build Word Power

Writing

Choose a spelling word and write an acrostic poem about your word. Let the spelling word be the *title* of the poem. Begin each line with a letter of the spelling word.

Growl
Grumbling and
rumbling, the
old lion
was guarding his
lair.

shout	blouse	thousand	clown	growl
proud	ounce	amount	drown	flower
sour	pound	eyebrow	howl	power

New Words
couch	prowl
tower	counter
sprout	surround
allow	

Reach Out for New Words

A Write the new **ou** or **ow** word that matches each meaning.
Then circle the **ou** or **ow** in each word.

1. to let

2. to be on all sides

3. start to grow

4. a long table top

5. to sneak

6. a tall, narrow building

7. a sofa

Writing

B Read each pair of sentences. Put the two sentences together to make one sentence that includes the underlined word.

1. Maple trees <u>surround</u> the house. Oak trees <u>surround</u> the house.

2. The <u>couch</u> is soft. The <u>couch</u> is comfortable.

3. Lions <u>prowl</u> in the jungle. Tigers <u>prowl</u> in the jungle.

4. I can see over the <u>counter</u>. The <u>counter</u> is in the office.

5. Tulips <u>sprout</u> in the spring. Daffodils <u>sprout</u> in the spring.

through

cough
bought
brought
thought
fought

dough
though

rough
enough

could
would
should
shoulder
boulder

1. What two letters do you see in every word?
2. What group of four letters do you see in ten of the words?
3. In how many words do the letters **ough** sound like **oo** in the word **too**? like **aw** in **paw**? like **o** in **go**? like **uff** in **cuff**?
4. What group of four letters do you see in five of the words?

Many words are spelled with the letter group **ough.**
This letter group can be pronounced in several different ways.
A few words are spelled with the letter group **ould.**

Practice the Words

A Write the spelling words that complete these sentences.

1. Tim went shopping and ____ some new socks.

2. ____ you like to come to my house for dinner?

3. Carol ____ some games to our party.

4. I ____ I heard the door creak open!

5. Jim tried, but he ____ not lift that heavy box.

6. Pete is making ____ for our pizza.

7. The two dogs ____ for the meaty bone.

8. Robin went swimming even ____ the water was cold.

9. You ____ wear knee pads when you skate.

10. Do we have ____ wood to build a clubhouse?

11. This gravel road is very ____ .

12. The train track runs ____ a tunnel in the mountain.

13. Football players wear helmets and ____ pads.

14. Smoke from the campfire made Ellen ____.

15. Sam sat on a huge ____ at the edge of the river.

B Add the missing letters to complete each word. Then write the word.

1. e __ o __ g __

2. b __ u __ h __

3. b __ u __ d __ r

4. t __ r __ u __ h

5. t __ o __ g __ t

6. d __ u __ h

7. s __ o __ l __ e __

8. c __ u __ h

9. c __ u __ d

C Write the two words that rhyme with each clue word and fit in the shapes.

1. caught

2. good

3. blow

4. stuff

Build Word Power

Follow the **+** and **−** signs to change each spelling word into another spelling word. All your spelling words are included in this exercise.

1. boulder **− b + sh** = _____ **− er** = _____

2. would **− w + c** = _____ **− ld + gh** = _____

3. dough **− d + r** = _____ **− r + en** = _____

4. brought **− r** = _____ **− b + f** = _____

5. through **− r** = _____ **+ t** = _____

through   brought   dough   enough   should
cough   thought   though   could   shoulder
bought   fought   rough   would   boulder

New Words
Discover
new words
below!

Reach Out for New Words

A Fifteen **ough** words are in this poem. Write the six new **ough** words that are not on your spelling list. Not all of the new words will be in heavy type.

I take it you already know
about **tough** and **rough**
And **cough** and **dough**,

And if you tried I know you could
Remember words
Like **would** and **should**.

Now if you don't, you really ought
To learn **although**
and **thought** and **fought**.

And so your list will really grow
Learn **trough** and **bought**
Thorough and **though**.

And if that's not enough for you
Then think of words
Like **sought** and **through**.

A silly language? I agree
How did we speak it
At the age of three?

I'm sure you know before I tell it
The problem now
Is how to spell it!

B Use each riddle to find one of your new **ough** words.

1. where horses drink; shaped like ☐☐☐☐☐

2. the antonym of **weak**; rhymes with **stuff**

3. has five letters; used instead of **should**

4. means the same as **looked for**; shaped like ☐☐☐☐☐☐

5. synonym for **but**; has two syllables

6. means **complete**; rhymes with **burrow**

73

10
holiday   holidays
chimney   chimneys
family   families

11
tiny   tinier   tiniest
busy   busier   busiest
friendly   friendlier   friendliest

12
try   trying   tried
reply   replying   replied
bury   burying   buried

13
drawing
lawn
crawling

14
autumn
because
taught

15
amount
growl
flower

16
thought
enough
would

A An analogy is a special way of showing how words go together. Look at the first pair of words in each row. In what way do these words go together? Write a spelling word that makes the second pair of words go together in the same way as the first pair.

1. **easy** is to **easier**   as   **tiny** is to _____

2. **try** is to **trying**   as   **reply** is to _____

3. **holiday** is to **holidays**   as   **chimney** is to _____

4. **try** is to **tried**   as   **bury** is to _____

5. **tiniest** is to **tiny**   as   **busiest** is to _____

6. **reply** is to **replies**   as   **family** is to _____

7. **tinier** is to **tiniest**   as   **busier** is to _____

8. **replied** is to **replying**   as   **tried** is to _____

Proofreading

B Find each misspelled word. Write the word correctly.

1. A small amownt of glue will be enuf.

2. I thougt Bill's house woud be easy to find.

3. Last year our familys spent the holidais together.

4. That building has two chimnies.

5. The baby is crauling, but he's not walking yet.

6. I like autum becaus of the cool weather.

C Complete each phrase with a word from the box.

growl	friendliest	taught	flower	holidays	replying
lawn	autumn	drawing	trying	buried	crawling

1. ____ the lesson

2. the ____ neighbors

3. smell the ____

4. heard the lion ____

5. ____ a picture

6. gold ____ leaves

7. mow the ____

8. ____ very hard

9. ____ to the question

10. celebrate the ____

11. ____ a bone

12. ____ on hands and knees

Using More Review Words

A Use the directions following each base word to make another form of the word.

1. **icy**   write the **est** form

2. **deny**   write the past tense

3. **study**   write the **ing** form

4. **silly**   write the **est** form

5. **library**   write the plural

6. **multiply**   write the past tense

7. **early**   write the **er** form

8. **country**   write the plural

9. **blueberry**   write the plural

10. **worry**   write the **ing** form

11. **empty**   write the past tense

12. **highway**   write the plural

13. **angry**   write the **est** form

14. **curly**   write the **er** form

15. **canary**   write the plural

B Three words in each row follow the same spelling pattern. One word does not. Find that word. Be ready to tell why it does not belong.

1. paw	claw	howl	straw
2. caught	brought	taught	daughter
3. dawn	shawl	law	clown
4. angrier	earliest	busier	icier
5. proud	should	would	could
6. duties	stories	countries	jockeys
7. sour	power	blouse	shout
8. haunt	launch	applaud	coleslaw
9. flurries	journeys	subways	displays
10. blouse	saucer	faucet	fault

C Complete these analogies. Write a word from the box that makes the second pair of words go together in the same way as the first pair.

author	rough	dawn	August	daughter
shawl	shoulder	boulder	claw	dough

1. **boy** is to **son** as **girl** is to ____
2. **person** is to **fingernail** as **animal** is to ____
3. **leg** is to **hip** as **arm** is to ____
4. **painting** is to **artist** as **book** is to ____
5. **January** is to **February** as **July** is to ____
6. **cake** is to **batter** as **bread** is to ____
7. **small** is to **large** as **pebble** is to ____
8. **silk** is to **smooth** as **sandpaper** is to ____
9. **head** is to **scarf** as **shoulders** are to ____
10. **evening** is to **sunset** as **morning** is to ____

cabin	dust	gloomy	rusty
rented	iron	scent	wooden
spooky	lamp	stairs	steep
curtains	mist	hinge	stove
damp	pine	lantern	bucket

Prewriting. Prewriting is the thinking and planning you do before you begin to write. In this lesson, you will plan and write a **description.** You will imagine or remember a scene. Then you will use sense details to share the sight and feeling with others.

Use Prewriting Skills

A Answer the questions with spelling words. The words will help you think of ways to describe an old house.

1. What kind of tree might you see outside the house?

2. What words make you think of wetness in the air? (2 words)

3. What words might describe the stairs? (2 words)

4. What words might describe an old door hinge? (2 words)

5. What words could describe the way the house feels to you? (2 words)

6. What might everything inside an old deserted house be covered with?

7. What specific household items might you see inside the house? (5 words)

8. What type of house could it be?

B Before you write, decide what feeling you want your description to have. The feeling might be happy, sad, scary, peaceful, or exciting. Choose your words to give this feeling.

Write the phrase from each pair that you would choose to create a scary feeling in your description.

1. rented a spooky cabin
   rented a log cabin

2. gloomy clouds
   bright sunshine

3. heavy, dark curtains
   clean, white curtains

4. smoky iron stove
   warm kitchen stove

5. sweet pine scent
   damp scent of mist

6. lantern glowing brightly
   lantern casting shadows

7. creaking rusty hinge
   shiny new hinge

8. wide, graceful stairs
   steep, narrow stairs

C Details in a description should be in a natural order that makes sense. Here are some examples of natural order:

tree—bottom to top
costume—top to bottom

surprise package—outside to inside
stage scene—left to right

Read this prewriting list of details describing a cabin. Decide on a natural order. Write the details in that order on your own paper.

rusty iron hinges swung open
cabin appeared spooky in the damp mist
creaky wooden stairs led to the front door
whole room inside felt dusty and gloomy
lantern hung just inside door

Now Think Make prewriting notes for your own paragraph about an old house. Use as many spelling words as you can. First decide what feeling your description will have. Then jot down what you can see through your senses. Finally, decide in what order you will give the details.

Use Writing Skills

A Complete each set of details with the correct spelling word.

Spelling Words

| lamp |
| stairs |
| cabin |
| curtains |
| stove |
| hinge |
| lantern |
| bucket |
| mist |
| scent |
| dust |
| pine |

Details

blackened, wood-burning _____

damp _____ creeping through the forest

steep _____ with creaking wooden boards

furniture covered with cobwebs and _____

charming, cozy log _____

rusty iron _____ on the door

white lace _____

_____ flickering in the wind

sharp needles of the _____ tree

heavy, metal _____ of sand

tall glass table _____

fragrant _____ of roses

B When you write a rough draft, you will have to expand your prewriting notes into sentences. Practice by expanding each phrase in Column 2 into a complete sentence. Use your own paper.

   Example: Dry twigs crackled inside the blackened, wood-burning stove.

Now Write

Look over your prewriting notes. Use them to write a paragraph about an old house. First think of a good topic sentence. Choose details by using your senses. Keep in mind the order in which you will describe things. Also think of the special feeling you want the reader to have. Use as many spelling words as possible.

Revising. One important part of revising is checking to see that you have avoided **run-on sentences.** A run-on sentence contains two or more complete thoughts that are run together.

Example: I tripped on the broken stairs the boards were rotten.

Separate run-on sentences with a punctuation mark. Mark the beginning of every new idea with a capital letter.

Example: I tripped on the broken stairs. The boards were rotten.

Use Revising and Proofreading Skills

A On your own paper, rewrite these run-on sentences correctly.

1. Dad rented a cabin in the woods it was made of logs and cement.
2. Mom shook the dust from the curtains they didn't look so gloomy now.
3. An old wooden bucket stood in the corner the bucket leaked a big puddle of water.
4. A thick mist rose from the ground drops of water clung to the pine needles.
5. There was a fresh scent of spring in the air I skipped happily down the steep front stairs.

B Proofread the following paragraph. Find the mistakes in capitalization, punctuation, and spelling. Then rewrite the paragraph.

Remember
- Use an exclamation point after a statement that shows strong feeling.
- Use an apostrophe to show where letters are left out in a contraction.
- Capitalize the names of people and pets.

Smoke poured from the chimney of the old cabin the wild wind howled around it. Rita and her dog sandy watched the sparks dance through the air. Suddenly the wodden roof caught fire. What a frightening sight that was Rita couldn't see because of the thick, gloomey smoke. she told sandy theyd have to go for help.

C Revise the following first draft. Then rewrite it correctly on your own paper. These directions will help you.

1. Find the sentence that is out of order.
2. Find the punctuation error in line 5.
3. Correct one capitalization error in line 4.
4. Find the run-on sentence. Add a punctuation mark and begin the next sentence with a capital letter.
5. Find the unnecessary word in line 3.
6. Find the six misspelled words. Write them correctly.

1   One peaceful autumn day Jeff sat outside the caben his family had

2   rented for the week.   After the bug flew away, he looked to the left.   First

3   he watched watched a frendly bug slowly crawling up the sleeve of his

4   jacket.   Then he saw his dog champ pick up the sent of a squirrel in the

5   nearby pine tree.   Ahead, he could see the red glow of a lanturn!   To his

6   right, he saw smoke slowly curling from the chimney next door.   His

7   nieghbor must be using the wood stoave for cooking.   He could almost

8   smell the aroma of her delicious ginger cookies.   Jeff yawned and closed

9   his eyes soon he was snoring.

Now Revise

Now read your own paragraph. Does each sentence tell about the main idea? Did you give details that can be observed through the senses? Are they in a natural order that makes sense? Does your description give a certain feeling to the reader? Have you used the best words? Remember to proofread for mistakes in capitalization, punctuation, and spelling. Then write your final copy in your best handwriting.

You've now written your own description. Trade descriptions with one of your classmates. Notice how each of you sees and describes things in a special, individual way.

A Writer's Journal

The paragraph below was written by a young girl. As you can tell, she has used her writing to express her personal thoughts and feelings. Her paragraph is a good example of one kind of journal entry that you, too, can write.

Read the paragraph in the box carefully. Then discuss the questions with your class.

1. How does the girl explain her changes in mood?
2. How do you think the girl would act when she is in her "good looks mood"? Her "loose end mood"?
3. Often, people have trouble finding the right words to explain what they are feeling or thinking. In your opinion, has the girl found the right words? Why do you feel the way you do?

Now use the paragraph as a starting point for your next journal entry. Here are some ideas for you.

1. Imagine what your mind is like inside. Tell how it looks and how it works.
2. Describe the mood you are in right now. Try to figure out what has caused you to feel the way you do.

Building a Personal Word List

Keeping a personal word list can help you become a better speller. First, you can easily see the words you need to learn to spell. Second, you can figure out the kinds of spelling errors you make.

Each time you enter words on your personal list, notice the kinds of spelling errors you made. Maybe you forgot to include the **h** when writing the words **chrome** or **rhyme**. You may begin to notice that you repeat the same kinds of spelling mistakes. If you know what kinds of spelling mistakes you make, you might be able to keep them from happening.

MY THOUGHTS

I sometimes wonder what my mind is like inside. Often I fancy that it is like this. I feel as if there is a ball in my mind and it is divided into pieces—each piece stands for a different mood. This ball turns every now and then and that's what makes me change moods. I have my learning mood, my good looks mood, my happy mood, my loose end mood and my grumpy mood, my miserable mood, my thoughtful mood and my planning mood. At the moment I am writing this I am in my thoughtful mood.

—SARAH GRISTWOOD

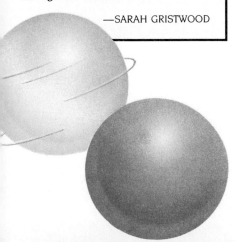

1 + 1 + 1 words and endings that begin with vowels

drip	*dripped*	*dripping*
grab	*grabbed*	*grabbing*
scrub	*scrubbed*	*scrubbing*
trip	*tripped*	*tripping*
trim	*trimmed*	*trimming*
clap	*clapped*	*clapping*
drag	*dragged*	*dragging*
step	*stepped*	*stepping*

1. Look at the words in the first column.
   How many syllables does each word have?
   How many vowels are in each word?
   How many consonants come at the end of each word?

2. The words in the second column are in the past tense.
   What two-letter ending was added to each of these words?
   Does the ending begin with a vowel or a consonant?
   What happened to the last letter of the base word when **ed** was added?

3. Look at the words in the last column.
   What three-letter ending was added to these words?
   Does the ending begin with a vowel or a consonant?
   What happened to the last letter of the base word when **ing** was added?

> Words that have 1 syllable and 1 vowel and end with 1 consonant
> are called **1 + 1 + 1 words**.
> Double the final consonant of a **1 + 1 + 1 word** before you add an
> ending that begins with a vowel, such as **ed** and **ing**.

A Complete each sentence with a spelling word. Use either the past tense or the **ing** form.

1. The audience is ____ loudly for the cast of the play.
2. John ____ over a rock and fell down.
3. The ant is ____ the bread crumb across the sidewalk.
4. The shortstop ____ the ball and threw it to home plate.
5. The barber is ____ my brother's hair.
6. I ruined my shoes when I ____ in the wet cement.
7. We called a plumber to fix the ____ faucet.
8. ____ an opponent is against the rules in football.
9. The sailor ____ the deck of the ship.
10. Avoid ____ in the mud.
11. My dog enjoys ____ a frisbee in her mouth.
12. ____ the floor is a tiring job.
13. The men ____ a huge log up the hill.
14. Ben ____ his hands in time with the music.
15. Rain ____ from the roof of our house.
16. The gardener ____ the trees and bushes.

B Unscramble each base word and write it. Then write its **ing** form.

1. prid
2. gard
3. brusc
4. ragb
5. pset
6. iptr

Dictionary

C Write the **ed** form of the spelling words in alphabetical order. Then write the **entry word** that you would look up in the dictionary to find the **ed** form.

Build Word Power

Writing

Write a sentence to answer each question. Use either the **ed** or **ing** form of the word in parentheses in your sentence.

1. How did Bobby skin his knee?   (trip)

2. Why are you calling the plumber?   (drip)

3. How did you get your sweater dirty?   (drag)

4. What work did you do in the yard today?   (trim)

5. How did you know the audience liked the play?   (clap)

6. Why are your tennis shoes wet?   (step)

dripped   grabbing   tripped   trimming   dragged   stepping
dripping   scrubbed   tripping   clapped   dragging
grabbed   scrubbing   trimmed   clapping   stepped

New Words
Discover
new words
below!

Reach Out for New Words

A Look at the words in each space. Write the eight words that follow the **1 + 1 + 1** spelling pattern.

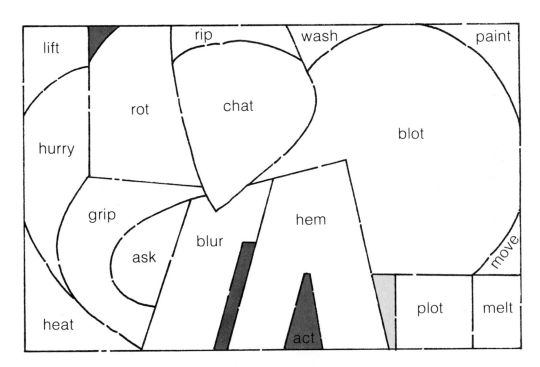

lift   rip   wash   paint
rot   chat
hurry   blot
grip
hem
blur   move
ask
plot   melt
heat   act

B Write the eight new **1 + 1 + 1** words in alphabetical order. Then write the past tense and **ing** forms of each word.

87

Lesson 20

1 + 1 + 1 words and endings that begin with consonants

bud	budd*ing*	bud*s*
clip	clipp*ing*	clip*s*
map	mapp*ing*	map*s*
snap	snapp*ing*	snap*s*
sad	sadd*er*	sad*ly*
thin	thinn*est*	thin*ly*
ship	shipp*ed*	ship*ment*
fit	fitt*ing*	fit*ness*

1. The words in the first column have ___ syllable and ___ vowel, and end with ___ consonant. They can be called ___ words.

2. Look at the words in the second column. What endings were added to make these words?
   Does each ending begin with a consonant or vowel?
   Was the final letter of the base word doubled when an ending was added?

3. Look at the words in the third column. What endings were added to make these words?
   Does each ending begin with a consonant or a vowel?
   Was the final letter of the base word doubled when an ending was added?

Do <u>not</u> double the final consonant of a **1 + 1 + 1 word** when you add an ending that begins with a consonant.

Practice the Words

A Use each clue to find a spelling word that fits in the puzzle.

Across
2. has buds growing
4. unhappily
5. drawings showing towns and streets
6. cutting
7. making something fit
9. slimmest
11. sent something from one place to another

Down
1. making a noise with your fingers
3. things that hold papers together
4. things that are shipped
5. drawing a picture of the earth
7. good health
8. in a thin way
10. small growths that will become flowers or leaves

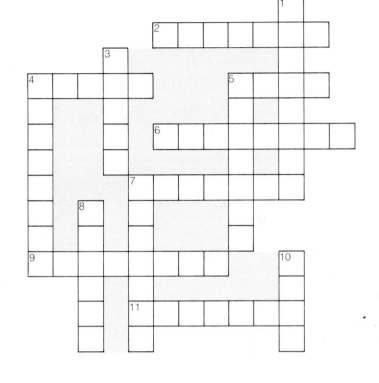

B Find the misspelled word in each group. Write the word correctly.

1. thinly
   buds
   sader
   snapping

2. clipping
   shippment
   maps
   fitting

3. shipped
   clips
   snapps
   budding

4. buds
   mapping
   thinest
   clips

5. maps
   sadley
   clipping
   shipped

6. thinly
   fittness
   fitting
   mapping

C Write the missing word in each phrase.

1. _____ trees
2. _____ of Michigan, Virginia, and Florida
3. _____ the puzzle pieces together
4. _____ by truck
5. flower _____
6. paper _____
7. the _____ on his jacket
8. _____ sliced bread
9. _____ a route
10. a newspaper _____
11. a _____ story
12. a _____ turtle

Build Word Power

Complete these analogies. Write a word that makes the second pair of words go together in the same way as the first pair. You may use spelling words or their base words.

1. **round** is to **flat**   as   **globe** is to _____
2. **wide** is to **narrow**   as   **thick** is to _____
3. **building** is to **strength**   as   **body** is to _____
4. **grass** is to **sprouting**   as   **flower** is to _____
5. **letter** is to **mailed**   as   **cargo** is to _____
6. **happily** is to **gladly**   as   **unhappily** is to _____
7. **hands** are to **clapping**   as   **fingers** are to _____
8. **cloth** is to **pins**   as   **paper** is to _____

budding	clips	snapping	sadly	shipped	fitness
buds	mapping	snaps	thinnest	shipment	
clipping	maps	sadder	thinly	fitting	

Reach Out for New Words

A Add the endings to each word. Then match each new word to its meaning.

1. cup + ful = ____   a happy feeling

2. slim + ness = ____   being thin

3. dim + ly = ____   as much as a cup will hold

4. glad + ness = ____   very heavy weights

5. ton + s = ____   not brightly

6. bag + ful = ____   narrow strips

7. strap + s = ____   in the wrong way

8. grim + ly = ____   as much as a bag will hold

9. bad + ly = ____   as much as a jar will hold

10. jar + ful = ____   in a harsh way

Dictionary

B Write the new words with the endings in alphabetical order. Look up each word in your spelling dictionary. It may be an entry word, or it may be part of the base word entry. Write all the other forms of the word that are included in the entry.

$$hop + ed = hopped$$
$$hope + ed = hoped$$

$$star + ing = starring$$
$$stare + ing = staring$$

$$tap + ed = tapped$$
$$tape + ed = taped$$

$$scar + ed = scarred$$
$$scare + ed = scared$$

$$cut + er = cutter$$
$$cute + er = cuter$$

$$plan + s = plans$$
$$plane + s = planes$$

$$cub + s = cubs$$
$$cube + s = cubes$$

$$tub + ful = tubful$$
$$tube + ful = tubeful$$

1. Some **1 + 1 + 1 words** and final **silent e** words look very much alike.
   The first word in each pair is a ___ word.
   The second word in each pair is a ___ word.

2. Which endings begin with a vowel?
   Which endings begin with a consonant?

3. What happened to the last letter of the base word when **ing**, **ed**, or **er**
   was added to a **1 + 1 + 1 word**?   to a **silent e** word?

4. What happened to the base word when **s** or **ful** was added
   to a **1 + 1 + 1 word**?   to a **silent e** word?

When you add an ending that begins with a vowel,
   the base word usually changes.
      The final **e** is dropped in final **silent e** words.
      The final consonant is doubled in **1 + 1 + 1 words**.
When you add an ending that begins with a consonant, the
   base word usually remains the same.

Practice the Words

A Complete each sentence with a spelling word.

1. The frightened rabbit _____ toward the woods.

2. My family _____ to go on a picnic this Sunday.

3. The tree trunk is _____ where it was struck by lightning.

4. Kim has always dreamed of _____ in a movie.

5. I _____ a note to the refrigerator door.

6. The paper _____ is very sharp, so be careful when you use it.

7. There are several trays of ice _____ in the freezer.

8. Lynn _____ Bob on the shoulder to get his attention.

9. The monster movie _____ me!

10. Hundreds of _____ land at the airport each day.

11. That little dog is _____ than the big brown one.

12. Sue was _____ at the acrobat on the high wire.

13. The mother bear protected her _____ .

14. Bob ran a _____ of water for his bath.

B Choose the correct spelling of each **base word + ending.** Then write the correct spelling.

1. **cut + er**	cuter	cutter
2. **scare + ed**	scared	scarred
3. **tube + ful**	tubeful	tubful
4. **tap + ed**	tapped	taped
5. **hope + ed**	hoped	hopped
6. **stare + ing**	starring	staring
7. **cute + er**	cutter	cuter
8. **scar + ed**	scared	scarred
9. **star + ing**	starring	staring

C Add the missing letters to complete each word. Then write the base word.

1. t a __ __ d

2. s t __ __ __ n g

3. h o __ __ d

4. c __ __ s

5. t u __ __ __ l

6. p l __ __ s

7. s c __ __ __ d

8. h o __ __ __ d

9. c u __ __ __ r

10. t u __ __ __ __ l

11. p l __ __ __ s

12. c __ __ __ s

Build Word Power

Writing

Write a sentence with each group of words below. Add an ending to at least one word in each sentence. Remember to think about the **1 + 1 + 1** and final **silent e** patterns when you add endings.

1. cute, stare, star

2. plan, hope, plane

3. tape, cut, tube

4. hop, scare, cub

hopped	staring	scarred	cuter	cubs	tubeful
hoped	tapped	scared	plans	cubes	
starring	taped	cutter	planes	tubful	

Reach Out for New Words

A Unscramble each group of letters to make a word. Then add the ending to each word. Check the spelling in the dictionary, and write the new word form.

1. peom _____ + ed = _____

2. opm _____ + ed = _____

3. orb _____ + ed = _____

4. boer _____ + ed = _____

5. praces _____ + s = _____

6. rascp _____ + s = _____

B Make two columns on your paper as shown below. Write each new base word in the first column. Write the meaning of each word in the second column so that it is *not* across from the correct word. Ask a friend to draw a line from each word to its meaning.

Words	**Meanings**
Example: **1.** scared	**a.** marked by an injury
2. scarred	**b.** frightened

95

badge
edge
bridge
dodge
fudge
judge

page
huge
stage
fringe
sponge
strange
garage
orange
arrange

1. Look at the first group of words. How many syllables
   does each word have?
   What are the last three letters of each word?
   Does a consonant or a vowel come before these letters?
   Is the vowel long or short?
2. Look at the second group of words. What are the last two
   letters of each word?

Use **dge** immediately after a single, short vowel in a one-syllable word.
Use **ge** in most other words.

A Use each clue to find the spelling words that fit in the boxes.

1. part of a book
2. a color
3. get out of the way
4. used to clean up spills
5. a border of hanging threads
6. keep a car in it
7. very large
8. where plays are performed
9. border
10. It goes over a river.
11. to put in order
12. a person who decides cases in a court of law

Proofreading

B Proofread this paragraph. Five of the words are misspelled. Find each misspelled word and write it correctly.

　　While working on a cooking bage for scouts, Jan and I made a huge batch of fudg. We found the recipe on padge fifteen of the cookbook. Jan got out the cocoa, salt, milk, butter, and vanilla. I got out a bowl, a mixer, and a spunge for cleaning up. As we mixed the ingredients, Jan took a taste from the edge of the bowl. He made a strang face. We had forgotten to add the sugar!

Dictionary

Each dictionary entry includes an abbreviation that tells you the part of speech of the entry word. Some parts of speech and their abbreviations are:

noun—*n.*   verb—*v.*   adjective—*adj.*

Some words have more than one part of speech listed in the entry.

huge (hyo͞oj) *adj.* very large —————————————— part of speech

judge (juj) *n.* an official who hears cases in a
law court and makes decisions on them
—*pl.* **judg′ es** ♦*v.* to hear cases and make
decisions in a law court } parts of speech

C Write your spelling words in alphabetical order. Look up each word in the dictionary. Write the abbreviation for the part or parts of speech you find in the entry.

Build Word Power

Each word below is part of a spelling word. Write the spelling word on the line. Do not use a spelling word more than once.

1. rag

2. tag

3. age

4. bad

5. ring

6. hug

7. rid

8. on

9. do

10. or

11. rang

12. range

badge	dodge	page	fringe	garage
edge	fudge	huge	sponge	orange
bridge	judge	stage	strange	arrange

Reach Out for New Words

A Words are printed in three directions in this puzzle. → ↓ ↘
Find three new **ge** words and four new **dge** words. Write each word.

c	q	p	t	j	c	h	h	j
s	h	r	l	s	h	p	r	s
u	n	a	z	e	e	f	g	m
b	w	d	l	o	d	g	e	u
m	f	x	d	l	g	g	k	d
e	z	b	k	c	e	l	e	g
r	e	x	c	h	a	n	g	e
g	q	m	p	g	v	m	g	w
e	b	r	n	s	t	l	x	e

B Use each clue to find one of the new words that fits in the puzzle.

Across
4. a dirty spot
7. dare

Down
1. a cabin
2. to put under water
3. trade
5. promise
6. a row of bushes

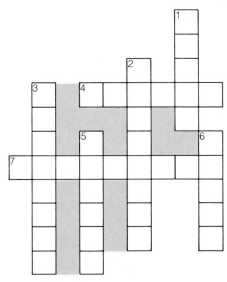

catch
patch
sketch
stretch
pitch
witch
ditch

touch
peach
beach
bench
march
sandwich
spinach
attach

1. Look at the first group of words.
How many syllables does each word have?
What are the last three letters of each word?
Does a consonant or a vowel come before these letters?
Is the vowel long or short?

2. Look at the second group of words.
What are the last two letters of each word?

Use **tch** immediately after a single, short vowel in a one-syllable word.
Use **ch** in most other words.

Practice the Words

A Use each clue to find a spelling word that fits in the puzzle.

Across
1. to draw
3. a long seat
5. a popular Halloween costume
7. to throw
9. to fasten together
10. to pull out of shape
11. to mend by adding a piece
12. a sandy shore
13. a steady walk

Down
1. slices of bread with filling between them
2. to capture
4. a green vegetable
6. to feel with the hand
8. a trench by a road
11. a fruit

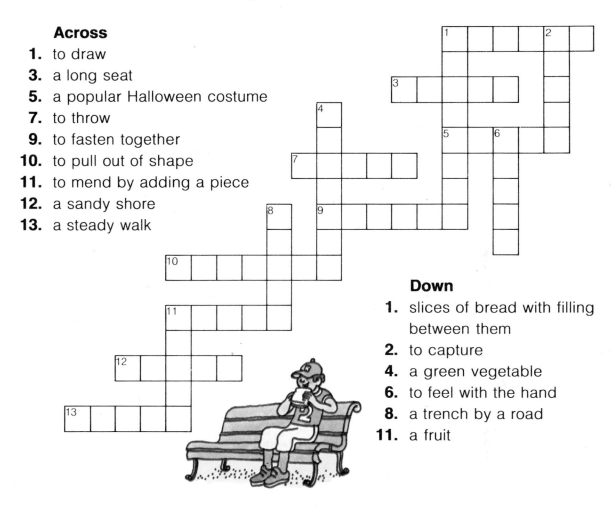

B Complete each sentence with spelling words that rhyme.

1. Mark ate a juicy _peach_ while sitting on the ____.

2. Try not to ____ the ball in the ____.

3. I will ____ out on the grass and ____ a picture.

4. Please ____ a ____ to these jeans before I ____ a cold!

Dictionary

Each dictionary entry tells the meaning, or **definition**, of the entry word.

C Write these words in alphabetical order. Look up each word in your spelling dictionary and write the definition.

witch touch peach bench sandwich march spinach

Build Word Power

Writing

Write a sentence with each group of words below. You may add the endings **ed**, **ing**, or **er** to some of the words if you wish.

1. pitch, catch, ditch

2. stretch, beach, sandwich

3. bench, sketch, peach

4. attach, patch, march

5. spinach, touch, witch

catch	stretch	ditch	beach	sandwich
patch	pitch	touch	bench	spinach
sketch	witch	peach	march	attach

Reach Out for New Words

Dictionary

A Copy the chart on your paper. Fill in **ch** or **tch** in each word below. Remember to use **tch** after a single, short vowel in a one-syllable word. Look up each word in your spelling dictionary. Write the word, the number of syllables, and the part or parts of speech.

	Word	Syllables	Part(s) of speech
1. cru _tch_	*crutch*	*1*	*n.*
2. approa ___			
3. sti ___			
4. swi ___			
5. dren ___			
6. ostri ___			
7. fe ___			
8. scra ___			

B Use the clues to write each new word that fits in the boxes.

1. a big bird
2. to go toward
3. to soak with water
4. to scrape with fingernails
5. to go and get
6. to sew
7. to exchange
8. a walking aid

bush + *es* = *bushes*
leash + *es* = *leashes*   *case* + *es* = *cases*
branch + *es* = *branches*   *fence* + *es* = *fences*
match + *es* = *matches*   *chance* + *es* = *chances*
ax + *es* = *axes*   *sentence* + *es* = *sentences*
waitress + *es* = *waitresses*   *sneeze* + *es* = *sneezes*
boss + *es* = *bosses*   *breeze* + *es* = *breezes*
circus + *es* = *circuses*   *package* + *es* = *packages*

1. The eight words in the first column are all singular nouns. How many words end with **sh**? with **ch**? with **x**? with **s**?
2. The seven **silent e** words are also singular nouns.
   How many end with **se**? with **ce**? with **ze**? with **ge**?
3. What ending was added to each singular noun to make the plural form?
4. What happened to the **silent e** when **es** was added?
5. Say the plural nouns. Each plural word has ___ more syllable than its singular form.

> When a word ends with **sh**, **ch**, **x**, or **s**, add **es** to make the plural form.
> When a word ends with **se**, **ce**, **ze**, or **ge**, drop the **e** and add **es** to make the plural form.
> A plural word that ends with **es** has one more syllable than its singular form.

A Write the spelling words that complete these sentences.

1. Clowns and trapeze artists perform at most ____.

2. The lumberjacks are using sharp ____ to chop wood.

3. The ____ served lunch to the customers.

4. All our neighbors have ____ around their yards.

5. Summer ____ help us keep cool.

6. The wind storm knocked four ____ off our tree.

7. Two big ____ arrived in the mail today.

8. Don wrote five ____ about the story.

9. I need ____ to light these candles.

10. Pat is trimming the ____ in our yard.

11. Our dogs enjoy going for walks on their ____.

12. Smelling pepper often causes ____.

B Find the misspelled word in each group. Write the word correctly.

1. fences	2. leashes	3. chanses
caces	branches	waitresses
sneezes	maches	bushes
axes	breezes	sentences

4. waitresses	5. sneezes	6. fences
breezes	boses	sentences
leashes	bushes	circusses
pakages	axes	branches

C Add the missing vowels to complete each word. Then write its base word.

1. s n __ __ z __ s

2. b __ s s __ s

3. b __ s h __ s

4. __ x __ s

5. c __ s __ s

6. f __ n c __ s

7. c h __ n c __ s

8. b r __ __ z __ s

9. c __ r c __ s __ s

10. b r __ n c h __ s

11. p __ c k __ g __ s

12. l __ __ s h __ s

13. w __ __ t r __ s s __ s

14. m __ t c h __ s

15. s __ n t __ n c __ s

Build Word Power

Each underlined word goes with one or more of your spelling words. Write the spelling word. Then write a sentence using both words.

1. Fire goes with ____ .

2. Clowns go with ____ .

3. Chopping goes with ____ .

4. Restaurants go with ____ .

5. Ribbons go with ____ .

6. Words go with ____ .

7. Trees go with ____ .

bushes	matches	bosses	fences	sneezes
leashes	axes	circuses	chances	breezes
branches	waitresses	cases	sentences	packages

New Words
Discover new words below!

Reach Out for New Words

A Find the correct path through this maze. Words that add **es** to make the plural form are on the correct path. Write the ten words that are on the correct path.

B Write the plural form of each new word you found in the maze.

nature
picture
capture
creature
future
fracture
pasture
mixture
lecture
signature
departure
furniture
adventure
temperature
manufacture

What are the last four letters of each word?

Many words end with the letters **ture.**

A Write your spelling words in alphabetical order. Then write the word or phrase in the sentence with almost the same meaning as the spelling word.

1. Exploring a cave is an exciting event.
2. Did the zoo keeper catch the lion?
3. A tiger is a beautiful living being.
4. The plane's leaving was delayed by snow.
5. Nick didn't break his arm when he fell out of the tree.
6. We bought new chairs and tables for our living room.
7. I hope to travel in space in the time to come.
8. The teacher gave a speech on sea life.
9. What do they make in that factory?
10. Hot chocolate is a combination of milk, sugar, and cocoa.
11. Fred hopes to become a famous outdoor photographer.
12. The cows are grazing in the field.
13. Ann took a photograph of the White House.
14. Is the artist's signed name on the painting?
15. Did the weather forecaster predict the degree of coldness for tomorrow?

B Write the spelling word that goes with each word or phrase.

1. exploring a sunken ship
2. a chair
3. *John Smith*
4. a broken leg
5. 1999
6. 75 degrees

Dictionary

C Write these words in alphabetical order. Then look up each word in your spelling dictionary and write the definition.

capture   pasture   lecture   manufacture   temperature   mixture

Build Word Power

Writing

Read each pair of sentences. Put the two sentences together to make one sentence that includes the <u>underlined</u> spelling word.

1. The teacher gave a <u>lecture</u>. The <u>lecture</u> was on early American settlers.

2. Mr. Clark bought some <u>furniture</u>. The <u>furniture</u> is made of oak.

3. Alice took a <u>picture</u>. The <u>picture</u> is of our family.

4. The cows are in the <u>pasture</u>. The <u>pasture</u> is behind the barn.

5. Jill stirred the <u>mixture</u>. The <u>mixture</u> is of butter, sugar, and eggs.

6. Terry enjoyed his <u>adventure</u>. His <u>adventure</u> was on board the ship.

nature   creature   pasture   signature   adventure
picture future   mixture   departure   temperature
capture fracture   lecture   furniture   manufacture

New Words

fixture
culture
posture
miniature
feature
agriculture
legislature
puncture

Reach Out for New Words

A Add the missing consonants to complete each word.
Then write the word.

1. _ ea _ u _ e

2. _ e _ i _ _ a _ u _ e

3. _ u _ _ _ u _ e

4. _ i _ _ u _ e

5. a _ _ i _ u _ _ u _ e

6. _ o _ _ u _ e

7. _ u _ _ u _ e

8. _ i _ ia _ u _ e

B Write the spelling words that complete these sentences.

1. Her eyes are the most beautiful ____ of her face.

2. Joshua has a collection of ____ cars.

3. Driving over a nail can ____ a tire.

4. It is interesting to study the ____ of other countries.

5. Improve your ____ by standing up straight.

6. The ____ of our country makes laws.

7. People who study ____ learn about farming.

8. A light ____ hangs above the dining room table.

19
drip   dripped   dripping
trim   trimmed   trimming
clap   clapped   clapping

20
sad   sadly
ship   shipment
fit   fitness

21
hop   hopped
hope   hoped
tape   taped

22
fudge
huge
orange

23
catch
peach
sandwich

24
bush   bushes
branch   branches
package   packages

25
picture
future
temperature

Using Review Words

A Complete these analogies. Write the spelling word that makes the second pair of words go together in the same way as the first pair.

1. **trim** is to **trimming**	as	**drip** is to ____
2. **thin** is to **thinly**	as	**sad** is to ____
3. **hope** is to **hoped**	as	**tape** is to ____
4. **trip** is to **tripped**	as	**clap** is to ____
5. **sandwich** is to **sandwiches**	as	**branch** is to ____
6. **tap** is to **tapped**	as	**hop** is to ____
7. **fitness** is to **fit**	as	**shipment** is to ____
8. **taped** is to **tape**	as	**hoped** is to ____
9. **oranges** is to **orange**	as	**packages** is to ____
10. **scrubbed** is to **scrub**	as	**trimmed** is to ____

Proofreading

B Find each misspelled word. Write the word correctly.

1. Carla raked the leaves and trimed the bushs.

2. In the fuchure, I will improve my physical fittness.

3. Jane ate a hudge bowl of fudge ripple ice cream.

4. These packages must be taped well for shippment.

5. Max hopped that Kate would give him a peech.

6. The rabbit hoped quickly into the woods.

C Complete each phrase with a word from the box.

picture	fudge	fitness	orange	temperature
sandwich	clapped	bushes	future	catch

1. ___ juice

2. ___ their hands

3. chocolate ___

4. ___ the ball

5. ham and cheese ___

6. painting a ___

7. ___ of 32°F

8. predict the ___

9. physical ___

10. trim the ___

Using More Review Words

A Use the directions following each base word to make another form of the word.

1. thin   write the **ly** form

2. thin   write the **est** form

3. scrub   write the past tense

4. leash   write the plural

5. step   write the **ing** form

6. sad   write the **er** form

7. fit   write the **ing** form

8. cut   write the **er** form

9. waitress   write the plural

10. trip   write the past tense

11. sentence   write the plural

12. tub   write the **ful** form

13. breeze   write the plural

14. drag   write the **ing** form

15. circus   write the plural

B Three words in each row follow the same spelling pattern. One word does not. Find that word. Be ready to tell why it does not belong.

1. touch   leash   beach   bench
2. page   badge   garage   arrange
3. scared   grabbed   clapped   scarred
4. nature   capture   pasture   stare
5. buds   fences   maps   snaps
6. bosses   axes   clips   matches
7. sentences   cases   chances   plans
8. stretch   drag   step   plan
9. attach   patch   witch   sketch
10. hoped   staring   tripping   cuter

C Complete these analogies. Write a word from the box that makes the second pair of words go together in the same way as the first pair.

beach	departure	planes	tubeful	stepping
axes	pitch	cubs	garage	spinach

1. **fingers** are to **snapping**   as   **feet** are to _____

2. **football** is to **pass**   as   **baseball** is to _____

3. **come** is to **go**   as   **arrival** is to _____

4. **jam** is to **jarful**   as   **toothpaste** is to _____

5. **sheep** are to **lambs**   as   **bears** are to _____

6. **cutting** is to **saws**   as   **chopping** is to _____

7. **river** is to **bank**   as   **ocean** is to _____

8. **drive** is to **buses**   as   **fly** is to _____

9. **airplane** is to **hangar**   as   **car** is to _____

10. **fruit** is to **apple**   as   **vegetable** is to _____

brand	facts	plenty	vitamins
money	ideas	healthy	cheaper
smart	goes	getting	product
truth	sale	forever	whether
until	cents	cereal	opinion

Prewriting. Prewriting is the thinking and planning you do before you begin to write. In this lesson, you are going to plan and write a **paragraph that explains why.** You will give reasons for an opinion.

Use Prewriting Skills

A Answer the questions with spelling words. The words will help you think of ideas for writing an ad or commercial for your favorite food.

1. What word means something that is made?

2. What word means the name on the label of a product?

3. What words might you use to talk about costs? (4 words)

4. What products can you buy at the grocery store? (2 words)

5. What should an honest advertisement tell? (2 words)

6. What word means "all that one needs"?

7. What should good food help you become?

8. When you say what brand you think is best, what are you stating?

B In a paragraph that explains why, you must give reasons. These reasons must be facts, not opinions. Facts can be proven right or wrong. Opinions cannot be proven. Read the six sentences below. Write three that are **opinions.**

1. Meowies Cat Food goes on sale today until Monday.

2. Shoppers with smart ideas should buy Meowies.

3. Once you buy Meowies, you will buy it forever.

4. Your pet will be getting vitamins and protein in its food.

5. Pets, whether young or old, should be fed Meowies.

6. Meowies is a product made from meat and natural foods.

C Plan to present your facts in order from the least to the most important. That way, your reader will be left with the strongest reason. Write the facts from Activity B in order from the least to the most important.

Now Think Make prewriting notes for your own magazine ad or TV commercial. Write about a food product such as cereal. Choose facts that will convince people to buy your product. Make up an imaginary brand name. Use as many spelling words as you can in your paragraph.

Use Writing Skills

A Write three different topic sentences that state opinions. Use the words in parentheses in each. Remember that opinions cannot be proven right or wrong.

1. (vitamins, healthy)　　**2.** (smart, brand)　　**3.** (product, cheaper)

B Do not combine more than two thoughts in one sentence. A sentence with three or more complete thoughts is called a **stringy sentence.**

> **Example:** Spotless Pans are made of metal and they have a non-stick surface and they are dishwasher safe.

Correct a stringy sentence by breaking it into at least two shorter sentences. Leave out one or more of the **and**'s. You may leave some ideas combined if they have a lot in common.

> **Example:** Spotless Pans are made of metal and they have a non-stick surface. They are dishwasher safe.

Rewrite these stringy sentences on your own paper. Be careful to use capital letters, commas, end marks, and connecting words in the right places.

1. Wisebuys is a paper that prints facts about new products and it gives good ideas on how to stay healthy and it only costs ninety cents.

2. You can find all brands of vitamins at the Smart Shop and we are open twenty-four hours a day and we even deliver.

Now Write

Use your prewriting notes to write an ad or commercial for a food product. Begin with a topic sentence that tells why your product is good. Then give facts that support your topic sentence. Arrange your facts from the least to the most important. Use as many spelling words as possible.

Revising. When you revise a paragraph that explains why, make sure that all your details are facts. These facts should support your topic sentence.

Use Revising and Proofreading Skills

A In the following paragraph, find two details that don't support the topic sentence. Also find one reason that is an opinion, not a fact. Rewrite the paragraph.

> Whether you feel healthy or not, you need to take Aunty Flynn's Vitamins every day. The Aunty Flynn brand is now over twenty years old. Aunty Flynn's has both Vitamin A and Vitamin C. It also contains minerals such as iron. Our vitamins are the best by far! Aunty Flynn's comes in a red box. Aunty Flynn's provides you with a daily supply of all the necessary vitamins.

B Proofread the following facts for mistakes in capitalization, punctuation, and spelling. Then write the sentences correctly.

Remember
- Use a comma before the word *and* when it connects two thoughts in a sentence.
- Do not combine more than two thoughts in a sentence.
- Capitalize brand names.

1. chewies is a new brand of sugarless gum. It helps to keep your mouth helthy and it adds plentey of shine to your teeth.

2. the big sale of supersuds Soap begins today and it will last until Friday during this time it will be cheiper than most other brands.

C Revise the following first draft. The directions below will help you. Then make a corrected copy on your own paper.

1. Find one reason that is an opinion, not a fact.
2. Correct one stringy sentence. Add a period and a capital letter. Drop one **and.**
3. Find six misspelled words. Write them correctly.
4. Correct the capitalization errors in lines 1 and 7.
5. Correct the punctuation errors in lines 1 and 5.

1   Laser Lights teaching Computer, is the best home computer ever

2 manufractured. It was designed by a team of engineers, teachers, and

3 students. This produck's memory center has all the facts you will need

4 and it has a homework input device, and their's a printer to deliver your

5 finished copy. Laser Lights works on laser beams and, that's why it's

6 cheeper to run than many other computers. This computer will look good

7 in your home. Most importantly, Laser lights is guaranteed farever. Call

8 555-2626 unntil midnight for more information. A salesperson will be glad

9 to give you a demonstration in your own home.

Now Revise

Read your own ad or commercial for a food product. Does your topic sentence give an opinion? Have you given at least three facts to back up the topic sentence? Are the facts stated in clear, short sentences? Check to make sure your statements are facts, not opinions. Then proofread for mistakes in capitalization, punctuation, and spelling. Make a final copy in your best handwriting.

Plan to read your paragraph aloud. Others will enjoy hearing how you have used the process of writing to express and support your opinion.

A Writer's Journal

Read the poem. Think about what it means. Then discuss the questions with your class.

1. At the first picnic were there really "tigers behind every boulder"?
2. By the second picnic, years later, what had changed? Had the rocks become smaller?

Maybe the poem or the discussion has given you a good idea for your next journal entry. If so, begin writing. If not, you might want to use one of the ideas given below.

1. Tell about a time when you imagined something scary. You might tell about something that happened a long time ago or something that happened recently. Try to figure out why you were scared.
2. Describe how you felt on your first day of school this year. Have your feelings changed between then and now? If so, why do you think they have changed? Answer these questions in your journal.

Building a Personal Word List

Your personal word list contains all the words that gave you trouble. Now that you know the words you need to practice, how can you go about learning these words? You could try one of these ways.

1. Look carefully at the words on your list. Do any of them look like words you know how to spell? Knowing how to spell **temperature** may help you spell **literature.**
2. Look for patterns. Do any of the words on your list have familiar spelling patterns? You might notice, for example, that **cases, fences,** and **breezes** all drop the silent **e** before the ending **es** is added. Practice spelling the words as a group.

GROWING UP

When I was seven
We went for a picnic
Up to a magic
Foresty place.
I knew there were tigers
Behind every boulder,
Though I didn't meet one
Face to face.

When I was older
We went for a picnic
Up to the very same
Place as before,
And all of the trees
And the rocks were so little
They couldn't hide tigers
Or *me* any more.

—HARRY BEHN

un + hurt   = unhurt
un + fold   = unfold
un + known   = unknown
un + popular   = unpopular
un + welcome   = unwelcome
un + important   = unimportant
un + lawful   = unlawful
un + friendly   = unfriendly
un + selfish   = unselfish
un + aware   = unaware
un + fastened   = unfastened
un + usual   = unusual

in + complete   = incomplete
in + correct   = incorrect
in + expensive   = inexpensive

A **prefix** is a group of letters added to the
beginning of a word to change its meaning.

1. What prefix was added to twelve of the base words?
2. What prefix was added to three of the base words?
3. Was the spelling of the base word changed when **un** or **in** was added?

The prefixes **un** and **in** mean *not* or *the opposite of*.
Do not change the spelling of the base word when a prefix is added.

    un + fold = unfold = the opposite of fold
    un + important = unimportant = not important
    in + correct = incorrect = not correct

Practice the Words

A The underlined words in each sentence have the same meaning as one of your spelling words. Write the spelling word.

1. My report is <u>not finished</u>.
2. Dad fell off the ladder, but he was <u>not injured</u>.
3. Anita is always <u>thoughtful of others</u>.
4. Please <u>spread out</u> the map so we can read it.
5. This type of music is <u>not liked by most people</u>.
6. These shirts are <u>not costly</u>.
7. Robbing banks is <u>not legal</u>.
8. The strange man was <u>not pleasant or agreeable</u>.
9. Mosquitoes are <u>not gladly allowed</u> in our house.
10. Your answer to this math problem is <u>wrong</u>.
11. This information was <u>of little value</u> to us.
12. The name of the person who wrote this poem is <u>not something we know</u>.
13. A solar eclipse is a <u>rare</u> event.
14. Todd <u>opened</u> the snaps on his jacket.

B Look at each word. If it is spelled correctly, draw a ☺. If it is misspelled, write the correct spelling.

1. unpopullar
2. unimportant
3. innexpensive
4. unlawfull
5. incorect
6. unusual
7. unfreindly
8. incorrect
9. unselfish
10. inccomplete
11. unawear
12. unfasened

Dictionary

C Write your **un** spelling words in alphabetical order. Then look up each word in the dictionary and divide it into syllables.

unaware un•a•ware

Build Word Power

Make at least three new words from each spelling word below by adding or subtracting prefixes and endings. You may use these endings: **s**, **ed**, **ing**, **ly**, and **less**.

1. unfold
2. unwelcome
3. unlawful
4. unfriendly
5. incomplete

unhurt unpopular unlawful unaware incomplete
unfold unwelcome unfriendly unfastened incorrect
unknown unimportant unselfish unusual inexpensive

New Words
Discover
new words
below!

Reach Out for New Words

A Write every other letter in each group below to find six new **un** words and two new **in** words. Always start by writing the second letter.

1. n i a n m d r i e g b e n s e t l i l o a n
2. a u i n c n r e a c m e v s e s c a h r i y
3. s u i n o e r x t p s e l c b t a e c d
4. c u o n g s h a c t d i n s a f l a n c r t f o n r b y
5. o i g n r c a o v n l s y i s d n e p r x a e t t e
6. n u e n l f l i a n v i o s l h r e m d
7. t u i n a p m r h e s p n a w r o e t d
8. c u i n l i a n d t n e a r l e r s d t n i o n w g

B Write the new word that matches each meaning.

1. not needed

2. not complete

3. not good enough

4. surprising

5. difficulty in digesting food

6. not of interest

7. not ready

8. not thinking of others

125

mis + spell = misspell
mis + understand = misunderstand
mis + behave = misbehave
mis + lead = mislead
mis + print = misprint
mis + lay = mislay
mis + read = misread
mis + used = misused

dis + obey = disobey
dis + arm = disarm
dis + like = dislike
dis + honest = dishonest
dis + please = displease
dis + loyal = disloyal
dis + connect = disconnect

1. A group of letters that is added to the beginning of a word to change its meaning is called a ___.
2. What two prefixes were added to the base words to make the words in the last column?
3. Was the spelling of the base word changed when the prefix was added?

> The prefix **mis** means *bad* or *wrongly.*
> The prefix **dis** means *not* or *to do the opposite.*
> Do <u>not</u> change the spelling of the base word when a prefix is added.
> mis + spell = misspell = to spell wrongly
> dis + obey = disobey = to not obey
> dis + connect = disconnect = the opposite of connect

Practice the Words

A Use each clue to find a spelling word that fits in the puzzle. The letter **s** has been given to help you.

1. to put in the wrong place
2. to take away weapons
3. used in the wrong way
4. lead in the wrong direction
5. not do as you are told
6. not enjoy
7. to read the wrong way
8. not faithful
9. to spell incorrectly
10. a mistake in printing
11. make someone angry
12. not truthful
13. to act badly
14. to break a connection
15. not get the meaning

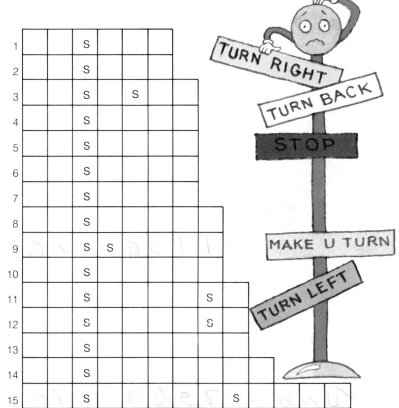

B Find the misspelled word in each group. Write the word correctly.

1. discconect
   disloyal
   mislead

2. dislike
   missunderstand
   misbehave

3. disarm
   mispell
   misprint

4. disarm
   mislay
   disonest

5. misused
   misread
   displeese

6. misbehave
   disobay
   disloyal

127

Dictionary

C Write your spelling words in alphabetical order. Remember to look at the fourth or fifth letter if the first letters are the same. Then look up each word in your spelling dictionary and write its part of speech.

Build Word Power

The words in the box are base forms of your spelling words. Use the clues to make new forms of these words. Make each new form by adding an ending or by adding both a prefix and an ending. Use the prefixes **mis** and **dis** and the endings **ly**, **ed**, and **s**. Write the new word forms that fit in the puzzle.

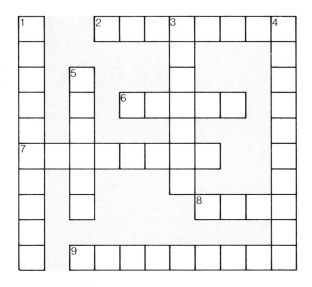

honest	like	behave	please	loyal
connect	lay	read	print	

Across
2. wasn't fond of
6. understands written words
7. in a truthful manner
8. puts down
9. joined two things together

Down
1. acted badly
3. in a faithful manner
4. made someone unhappy
5. writes the letters of the alphabet

misspell   mislead misread disarm   displease
misunderstand misprint misused dislike   disloyal
misbehave   mislay   disobey dishonest disconnect

New Words
orderly
trust
treat
conduct
informed
quoted
obedient

Reach Out for New Words

A Use the code to find the **mis** or **dis** form of each word.
Each number stands for one letter of the alphabet.
Decode each word and write it.

j	q	f	m	a	i	s	c	g	r	x	b	z	h
1	2	3	4	5	6	7	8	9	10	11	12	13	14

u	p	d	k	o	y	t	e	l	w	v	n
15	16	17	18	19	20	21	22	23	24	25	26

1. __4__ __6__ __7__ __21__ __10__ __22__ __5__ __21__
2. __17__ __6__ __7__ __21__ __10__ __15__ __7__ __21__
3. __17__ __6__ __7__ __19__ __10__ __17__ __22__ __10__ __23__ __20__
4. __17__ __6__ __7__ __19__ __12__ __22__ __17__ __6__ __22__ __26__ __21__
5. __4__ __6__ __7__ __8__ __19__ __26__ __17__ __15__ __8__ __21__
6. __4__ __6__ __7__ __2__ __15__ __19__ __21__ __22__ __17__
7. __4__ __6__ __7__ __6__ __26__ __3__ __19__ __10__ __4__ __22__ __17__

B Write the new **mis** and **dis** words in alphabetical order. Then find a word or
phrase with the same meaning in the sentence.

1. Bill enrolled his puppy in dog training class because
   his puppy was refusing to do as told.
2. Jill couldn't find her notebook in her messy desk.
3. Do you doubt the person who borrowed money from you?
4. Ann's bad behavior surprised everyone.
5. Lee gave the wrong facts to Ted about the class picnic.
6. The reporter repeated incorrectly the words of the mayor.
7. If you don't hurt this watch, it should last ten years.

Possessive form of singular nouns

teacher	teacher's
student	student's
coach	coach's
principal	principal's
captain	captain's
pilot	pilot's
dentist	dentist's
clerk	clerk's
waiter	waiter's
chef	chef's
hawk	hawk's
tiger	tiger's
spider	spider's
elephant	elephant's
camel	camel's

The **possessive form** of a noun shows ownership or possession.

1. What was added to each singular noun in the first column
   to make the possessive form in the second column?
2. Was the spelling of the base word changed when **'s** was added?

Make the possessive form of a singular noun by adding **'s.**
Do <u>not</u> change the spelling of the base word when you add **'s.**
   tail of the tiger = the tiger's tail

Practice the Words

A Rewrite each phrase. Use the possessive form of the underlined word.

1. the paws of the <u>tiger</u>   *the tiger's paws*
2. the tray of the <u>waiter</u>
3. the airplane of the <u>pilot</u>
4. the chair of the <u>dentist</u>
5. the eyelashes of the <u>camel</u>
6. the office of the <u>principal</u>
7. the cash register of the <u>clerk</u>
8. the legs of the <u>spider</u>
9. the wings of the <u>hawk</u>
10. the recipe of the <u>chef</u>
11. the pencil of the <u>student</u>
12. the uniform of the <u>captain</u>

B Complete each phrase with a possessive spelling word. Write each word only once.

1. ___ feathers
2. ___ homework
3. ___ web
4. ___ hump

5. ___ school
6. ___ class
7. ___ striped fur
8. ___ parachute

9. ___ trunk
10. ___ football team
11. ___ ship
12. ___ drill

Proofreading

C Proofread these sentences. Find each misspelled word. Write the word correctly.

1. He asked for the clerks's help in choosing his teache'rs gift.

2. A tiger's paws are smaller than an elephants feet.

3. The waiters's tray can hold six pieces of the chefs fresh pie.

4. The principals's speech was about bicycle safety.

5. Our coachs' advice was the same as our team captain's.

Build Word Power

Other singular words can also show possession.

> my   mine   your   yours   her   hers   his   its

These words are called **possessive pronouns**.
Possessive pronouns do not have an apostrophe.
Possessive pronouns can be used in place of possessive nouns.

> The spider is spinning *the spider's* web.
> The spider is spinning *its* web.

Find the possessive noun in each sentence. A possessive pronoun could take its place. Write the possessive pronoun.

1. The pilot, Fred Estrada, buckled the pilot's safety belt.

2. The camel can carry a load on the camel's back.

3. Kathy said to the coach, "I think this ball is the coach's."

4. The student said, "That book is the student's."

5. Our teacher, Ms. Jones, let us borrow the teacher's book.

6. Mr. Jackson said to the chef, "May I have the chef's secret recipe?"

teacher's principal's dentist's chef's spider's
student's captain's clerk's hawk's elephant's
coach's pilot's waiter's tiger's camel's

New Words

treasurer squirrel
artist gymnast
secretary president
reporter

Reach Out for New Words

A Write the possessive forms of the new words in alphabetical order. Then write a phrase with each one. The first one is done to show you.

1. _artist's_   _the artist's canvas_

Writing

B Rewrite each sentence, using the possessive form of the underlined word.

1. This notebook belongs to the <u>reporter</u>.

2. Nuts are the favorite food of the <u>squirrel</u>.

3. The trophy belongs to the <u>gymnast</u>.

4. This painting is the best work of the <u>artist</u>.

5. The typewriter of the <u>secretary</u> is broken.

6. Tim is the campaign manager of the class <u>president</u>.

7. Keeping track of money is the job of the <u>treasurer</u>.

Possessive form of plural nouns

farmers	farmers'
doctors	doctors'
nurses	nurses'
sailors	sailors'
ladies	ladies'
plants	plants'
animals	animals'
horses	horses'
mountains	mountains'
trains	trains'
teams	teams'
families	families'
men	men's
women	women's
children	children's

1. The words in the first column are plural nouns.
   How many end with **s**? How many do not end with **s**?

2. The words in the last column are the possessive forms of the plural nouns.
   What was added to the nouns that end with **s**?
   What was added to the nouns that do __not__ end with **s**?

> When a plural noun ends with **s**, add only an apostrophe
>   to make the possessive form.
> When a plural noun does not end with **s**, add **'s** to make
>   the possessive form.
>
>   crops that belong to the farmers = the farmers' crops
>   toys that belong to the children = the children's toys

Practice the Words

A Use each clue to find a spelling word that fits in the puzzle. Remember to count a space for the apostrophe.

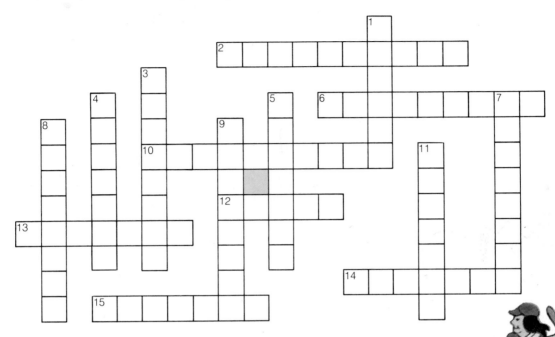

Across
2. belongs to the children
6. belongs to the families
10. of the mountains
12. belongs to the men
13. of the horses
14. belongs to the nurses
15. belongs to the women

Down
1. belongs to the teams
3. belongs to the farmers
4. of the plants
5. of the trains
7. belongs to the sailors
8. belongs to the doctors
9. of the animals
11. belongs to the ladies

B Write the possessive form of the underlined word.

1. friends of the <u>children</u>
2. umbrellas of the <u>men</u>
3. uniforms of the <u>sailors</u>
4. luggage of the <u>ladies</u>
5. engines of the <u>trains</u>
6. hats of the <u>women</u>

C Below are names of owners and the things they own. Write a phrase with each pair of words. Use the possessive form of each underlined word.

	Thing	Owner		Thing	Owner
1.	office	doctors	**6.**	peaks	mountains
2.	uniforms	teams	**7.**	caps	nurses
3.	land	farmers	**8.**	fur	animals
4.	houses	families	**9.**	hoofs	horses
5.	leaves	plants			

Build Word Power

Possessive pronouns can also show possession.
     our   ours   your   yours   their   theirs

Possessive pronouns do <u>not</u> have an apostrophe.
Possessive pronouns can be used in place of possessive nouns.

    The doctors opened *the doctors'* new office.
    The doctors opened *their* new office.

Find the possessive noun in each sentence. A possessive pronoun could take its place. Write the possessive pronoun.

1. The sailors are docking the sailors' ship.

2. The police officer said to the men, "Is this car the men's?"

3. The children told me that those toys are not the children's.

4. Mr. McDonald said, "The other farmers and I are worried that insects will destroy the farmers' crops."

5. The doctors said, "This new office is the doctors'."

6. Karen said to the horses, "I'll bring the horses' food soon."

farmers' sailors' animals', trains' men's
doctors' ladies' horses' teams' women's
nurses' plants' mountains' families' children's

New Words

carpenter   astronaut
company   hotel
officer   scientist
workman

Reach Out for New Words

A Copy the chart on your paper. Write your seven new words in alphabetical order on this chart. Follow the directions at the top of each column.

Singular Form	Plural Form	Possessive Form of the Plural
astronaut	*astronauts*	*astronauts'*

B Rewrite each phrase using the possessive form of the underlined word.

1. saws of the <u>carpenters</u>

2. tools of the <u>workmen</u>

3. guests of the <u>hotels</u>

4. spacesuits of the <u>astronauts</u>

5. microscopes of the <u>scientists</u>

6. offices of the <u>companies</u>

7. uniforms of the <u>officers</u>

table
ankle
tickle
candle
purple
turtle
simple
handle
couple
pickle
people
marble
double
buckle
trouble

1. What are the last two letters of each word?
2. Is the letter before **le** a vowel or a consonant?

Many words end with a **consonant + le**.

138

Practice the Words

A Use each riddle to find a spelling word. Write the word.

1. a part of the leg; shaped like

2. a piece of furniture; has five letters

3. a stick of wax; rhymes with **handle**

4. synonym for **pair;** shaped like

5. worry; has seven letters

6. part of a belt; rhymes with **chuckle**

7. a color; shaped like

8. twice as much; rhymes with **trouble**

9. humans; rhymes with **steeple**

10. an animal; shaped like

11. flavored with dill; shaped like

12. synonym for **easy;** rhymes with **dimple**

13. it makes you laugh; shaped like

14. part of a cup; rhymes with **sandal**

B Answer each question with spelling words. You will use some words more than once.

1. Which words end with **ckle**?

2. Which words end with **ple**?

3. Which words end with **ble**?

4. Which words have the letters **an**?

5. Which words have the letter **r**?

Dictionary

Some words have more than one meaning, or definition, listed in the dictionary. Each definition is given a number.

ta·ble (tā′b'l) *n.* ① a piece of furniture with a flat top set on legs. ② a chart of facts and figures. definition numbers

C Complete each sentence with a word from the box. Look up each word in your spelling dictionary. Write the number of the meaning that was used in the sentence.

double   table   marble

1. Put the dishes on the ___*table*___ .   _1_

2. The statue is made of ___ .   _____

3. The population of our town may ___ in ten years.   _____

4. I am studying the multiplication ___ .   _____

5. The clear, blue ___ is Harry's favorite.   _____

6. I hope Don will ___ when it's his turn to bat.   _____

Build Word Power

Write new forms of your spelling words. Remember that your spelling words end with **silent e**.

1. tickle; **ing** form ___*tickling*___

2. turtle; plural

3. marble; plural

4. table; **ful** form

5. buckle; **ing** form

6. couple; plural

7. simple; **er** form

8. handle; **er** form

9. double; **ed** form

10. ankle; plural

11. trouble; **ed** form

12. simple; **est** form

13. candle; plural

14. pickle; **ing** form

table	candle	simple	pickle	double
ankle	purple	handle	people	buckle
tickle	turtle	couple	marble	trouble

New Words
Discover new words below!

Reach Out for New Words

A Find the correct path through this maze. Words that end with a **consonant + le** are on the correct path. Write the eight words that are on the correct path.

START ········· sample ········· sprinkle ·······

····· shovel ·····

····· smile ··········· pencil··· ···animal·

········· jungle ·······

····· snail ······· single ·····

··· twirl ··· castle ····· snarl·

twinkle ·· wrestle ·····

· hotel··········· dimple···········

········ beautiful ······· scale ·····

FINISH

B Write four silly sentences using two or more **consonant + le** words in each sentence. Use all your new **consonant + le** words. You may add endings to the words if you wish. You may also use base list words. Circle the **consonant + le** words in each sentence. An example is done to show you.

My pet turtle sampled the pickle.

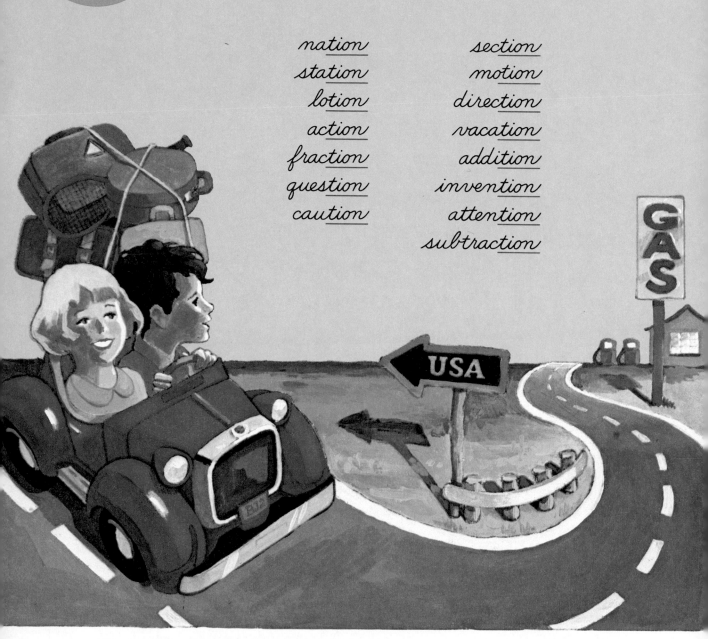

nation   section
station   motion
lotion   direction
action   vacation
fraction   addition
question   invention
caution   attention
                subtraction

What are the last four letters of each word?

Many words end with the letters **tion**.

Practice the Words

A Use each clue to find a spelling word that fits in the puzzle. Some of the letters have been given to help you.

1. a place to meet a train

2. North, South, East, or West

3. hand cream

4. a new gadget

5. subtracting one number from another

6. a country

7. an act

8. keeping your mind on something

9. 1/4

10. a separate part

11. movement

12. adding numbers

The puzzle column reads (top to bottom): t, i, o, n, t, i, o, n, t, i, o, n

B Add the missing vowels to complete each word. Then write the word.

1. s __ c t __ __ n

2. __ c t __ __ n

3. n __ t __ __ n

4. l __ t __ __ n

5. f r __ c t __ __ n

6. __ n v __ n t __ __ n

7. __ t t __ n t __ __ n

8. d __ r __ c t __ __ n

9. __ d d __ t __ __ n

10. m __ t __ __ n

11. s __ b t r __ c t __ __ n

143

Dictionary

Many words have more than one part of speech listed in the dictionary. For each part of speech there may be several definitions. These are numbered starting with **1**.

ques·tion (kwes′ chən) *n.* **1** something asked. ⟩two noun definitions
2 a matter to be considered; problem. ◆*v.* to ____one verb definition
ask questions of.

C Complete each sentence with a word from the box. Look up each word in your spelling dictionary. Write the part of speech and the number of the meaning that was used in the sentence.

question station vacation caution	Part of Speech	Meaning

1. Our teacher will ___*station*___ a monitor here.   *v*
2. Do you have a ____ about this lesson?   ____ ____
3. Please ____ Jill about the broken step.   ____
4. I have three days of ____ coming soon.   ____
5. The Bonatas will ____ in Europe.   ____
6. What is your favorite radio ____?   ____ ____
7. The police officer will ____ the suspect about the robbery.   ____
8. Use ____ when you climb the tree.   ____

Build Word Power

Write **concrete poems** with two or more of your spelling words. Make a shape with each word that reminds you of its meaning.

nation	action	caution	direction	invention
station	fraction	section	vacation	attention
lotion	question	motion	addition	subtraction

New Words

imagination
punctuation
instruction
multiplication
definition
suggestion
information

Reach Out for New Words

A Unscramble each group of syllables to make a word.
There is one extra syllable in each group.

1. ma   ges   for   tion   in

2. ti   tion   tu   ca   pli   mul

3. tion   mag   ges   sug

4. i   for   tion   def   ni

5. struc   in   tion   par

6. tu   a   ma   tion   punc

7. i   tion   sug   i   mag   na

Writing

B Many of the new words could be used to write a paragraph about school.
> Study the multiplication table . . .
> Use your imagination . . .

Pretend you are a teacher. On another sheet of paper, write out some
instructions you might give your class. Try to use all your new words. You may
use the plural form of some words if you wish.

apart + ment = apart*ment*

base + ment = base*ment*

pave + ment = pave*ment*

amuse + ment = amuse*ment*

excite + ment = excite*ment*

measure + ment = measure*ment*

improve + ment = improve*ment*

sad + ness = sad*ness*

ill + ness = ill*ness*

soft + ness = soft*ness*

kind + ness = kind*ness*

fair + ness = fair*ness*

happy + ness = happ*iness*

polite + ness = polite*ness*

crunchy + ness = crunch*iness*

What two suffixes were added to the base words to make the words in the last column?

The suffixes **ment** and **ness** are added to words to form nouns.

A Write the spelling words that complete these sentences.

1. We live in an ＿＿ on the third floor of this building.

2. Jake is recovering from a serious ＿＿ .

3. Everyone was satisfied with the ＿＿ of the rules.

4. I like to feel the ＿＿ of a kitten's fur.

5. Michele always treats animals with ＿＿ .

6. The ＿＿ of our house flooded during the rainstorm.

7. The ＿＿ is so hot that it burns the bottoms of your feet.

8. Bob felt great ＿＿ when his best friend's family moved to another town.

9. Rosa's smile showed her ＿＿ at winning the award.

10. We need an accurate ＿＿ of the length of this room.

11. I love the ＿＿ of a football game!

12. To Ron's ＿＿ , the funhouse mirror made him look two feet tall.

B Copy the chart on your paper. Look at the base words on your spelling list. Look for **1 + 1 + 1**, **silent e**, and **consonant + y** words. Then complete the chart.

	base word	ment/ness form
1 + 1 + 1		
silent e		
consonant + y		

147

C Unscramble each base word. Write each word. Then write its **ment** or **ness** form.

1. ceetix
2. lil
3. fots
4. irfa
5. knid
6. praat

7. seemura
8. esuma
9. pypha
10. vripeom
11. pletio
12. chynurc

Build Word Power

Writing

A **cinquain** is a poem that has five lines.

Line 1: a noun   Pavement

Line 2: two describing words that   Hard, rough
go with the noun

Line 3: three action words that   Walking, running, skipping
go with the noun

Line 4: four words giving a thought   Pathway to new places
or feeling about the noun

Line 5: another noun that goes with   Sidewalk
the first noun

Write two cinquains. The first word in each cinquain should be a spelling word.

apartment amusement improvement softness happiness
basement   excitement   sadness   kindness politeness
pavement   measurement illness   fairness crunchiness

New Words
equip
lovely
entertain
lonely
develop
tender
gentle

Reach Out for New Words

A Find the **ment** or **ness** form of each new word in this puzzle.
Write each word.

road developmententertainmenta
loveliness
lonely
gentleness tenderness list ilossen
nessafeequipmento

B Each sentence will remind you of one of the new **ment** or **ness** words. Write
the word that each sentence describes.

1. The steak can be easily cut with a fork.
2. The woman's face was beautiful.
3. Jan's friends were away for the summer.
4. Greg stroked the kitten's fur.
5. The band played and we danced.
6. We took a tent, a stove, a hatchet, and a
lantern on our camping trip.
7. Fred's skill as a writer improves daily.

28

friendly unfriendly
complete incomplete
expensive inexpensive

29

understand misunderstand
like dislike
honest dishonest

30

teacher teacher's
coach coach's
dentist dentist's

31

teams teams'
families families'
children children's

34

amuse amusement
excite excitement
kind kindness

32

table
candle
double

33

question
vacation
addition

A Complete these analogies. Write a spelling word that makes the second pair of words go together in the same way as the first pair.

1. **expensive** is to **inexpensive**　as　**complete** is to ____

2. **amuse** is to **amusement**　as　**excite** is to ____

3. **pilot** is to **pilot's**　as　**dentist** is to ____

4. **behave** is to **misbehave**　as　**understand** is to ____

5. **coach** is to **coach's**　as　**teacher** is to ____

6. **dislike** is to **like**　as　**dishonest** is to ____

7. **men** is to **men's**　as　**children** is to ____

8. **teams** is to **teams'**　as　**families** is to ____

9. **soft** is to **softness**　as　**kind** is to ____

10. **unlawful** is to **lawful**　as　**unfriendly** is to ____

Proofreading

B Cross out each misspelled word. Write the word correctly.

1. The dentist's new office adition is still incomplete.

2. Both teams's uniforms are the same color.

3. I disslike people who are disonest.

4. We will visit an amusment park during our vaction.

5. I'm surprised that this record is innexpensive.

6. The unfreindly dog frightened me.

C Complete each phrase with a word from the box.

table	coach's	candle	vacation	amusement
question	double	children's	kindness	addition

1. light the ____
2. ask a ____
3. ____ and subtraction
4. the ____ game plan
5. summer ____

6. set the ____
7. the ____ toys
8. a ____ dip ice cream cone
9. ____ to animals
10. smiled in ____

Using More Review Words

A Use the directions following each base word to make another form of the word.

1. women — write the possessive form
2. fold — write the **un** form
3. improve — write the **ment** form
4. spell — write the **mis** form
5. principal — write the possessive form
6. important — write the **un** form
7. connect — write the **dis** form
8. obey — write the **dis** form
9. happy — write the **ness** form
10. sad — write the **ness** form
11. ladies — write the possessive form
12. selfish — write the **un** form
13. correct — write the **in** form
14. measure — write the **ment** form
15. trains — write the possessive form

152

B Three words in each row follow the same spelling pattern. One word does not. Find that word. Be ready to tell why it does not belong.

1. action   nation   caution   simple
2. disloyal   purple   pickle   handle
3. misbehave   displease   unhurt   soft
4. captain's   plants'   camel's   pilot's
5. illness   measurement   misprint   fairness
6. tiger's   sailors'   doctors'   farmers'
7. lotion   unknown   fraction   station
8. couple   double   turtle   trouble
9. men's   women's   mountains'   children's
10. pavement   basement   improvement   apartment

C Complete these analogies. Write a word from the box that makes the second pair of words go together in the same way as the first pair.

basement	direction	mountains	station	incorrect
spider's	tiger's	pilot's	ankle	nation

1. **airplane** is to **airport**   as   **train** is to _____
2. **right** is to **correct**   as   **wrong** is to _____
3. **bus** is to **driver's**   as   **plane** is to _____
4. **spots** are to **leopard's**   as   **stripes** are to _____
5. **hand** is to **wrist**   as   **foot** is to _____
6. **hive** is to **bee's**   as   **web** is to _____
7. **low** is to **valleys**   as   **high** is to _____
8. **above** is to **attic**   as   **below** is to _____
9. **Boston** is to **city**   as   **United States** is to _____
10. **red** is to **color**   as   **north** is to _____

153

desk pencil stamp wonderful
gift crayon truly envelope
neat period front present
line been space delivered
left given blank remembered

Prewriting. Prewriting is the thinking and planning you do before you begin to write. In this lesson, you are going to plan and write a **friendly letter.**

Use Prewriting Skills

A Answer the questions with spelling words. The words will help you think about letter writing.

1. What synonyms are things you would write to thank someone for? (2 words)

2. What two objects are needed to mail a letter?

3. What word follows **Yours** in a letter closing?

4. What word tells how a letter should look?

5. What two words together mean an empty place on a page?

6. What noun means a writing place?

7. What verbs could be used after **has been** or **have been** in a letter? (4 words)

8. What word is a punctuation mark you will use?

B Your letter should have five main parts:

1. heading (your address and the date)
2. greeting (a simple way of saying "hello")
3. body (details you write)
4. closing (simple way of saying "goodbye")
5. signature (your handwritten name)

Use spelling words to complete these sentences. They contain other facts you need to know about writing a letter.

1. Use a ZIP code so your letter can be _____ easily.

2. Plan to write in ink, not _____ or _____.

3. Begin the greeting on the _____ side of the page.

4. Indent the first _____ of each paragraph.

5. Write the correct address and put a stamp on the _____ of the _____.

C You may plan to write a friendly letter for several reasons. You may want to share news or thank someone. You may want to give or accept an invitation. Read these phrases and decide whether they belong in a thank-you letter or an invitation. Write each phrase under the correct heading.

a wonderful present
surprise party will be given
bring a small gift

we'll meet in front
has been delivered safely
thank you for remembering

Thank-You Letter   **Invitation**

Now Think   Make prewriting notes for the content of your own letter to a friend. Decide what kind of letter you will write. Be sure to include enough details or information.

Writing. Use different types of language in different situations. When you write to a close friend, use informal or everyday language. When you write to adults or strangers, use more formal language. Carefully choose words that everyone will understand. Avoid slang.

Use Writing Skills

A Read the following pairs of sentences. Each pair expresses the same idea. Write the sentence in each pair that uses more formal language.

  1. Hey, man, how's tricks?
     Tell me, Tom, how have you been?
  2. Thank you for the wonderful game!
     Thanks for the neat game!
  3. How about coming to a show next weekend?
     I truly hope you can attend a theater party next weekend.
  4. I'll look forward to your delicious refreshments.
     I'll be first in line for the goodies.
  5. It's so cool that you remembered my birthday.
     It was thoughtful of you to have remembered my birthday.

B Rewrite the following sentences on your own paper. Replace the underlined slang words or expressions with more formal language.

  1. That meal I cooked left me feeling gross.
  2. Your handmade card and envelope were really intense!
  3. We signed up at the desk for the freebies.
  4. I thought I remembered your number, but I drew a blank.
  5. That glow-in-the-dark pencil was really neat.

Now Write   Look over your prewriting notes. Use them to write a letter to a friend. Remember to include all five parts of a letter. Talk about yourself, but also ask questions. Choose language that fits the situation.

Revising. When you revise your letter, make sure that every sentence expresses a complete thought.

Use Revising and Proofreading Skills

A When you write to friends, thoughts may come faster than you can put them down on paper. You may leave out either the beginning or the ending of a sentence. For example, *the pretty gray sweater* does not tell *who* or *what happened*. Here are two ways to complete this *sentence fragment*.

> I really love <u>the pretty gray sweater</u>.
> <u>The pretty gray sweater</u> fits just fine.

Add words to make a complete sentence of each fragment below. Write each complete sentence on your own paper.

1. the truly useful desk set
2. his big stamp collection
3. the ZIP code on the envelope
4. a huge red crayon
5. their front door

6. your wonderful present
7. those long lines for the rides
8. the automatic pencil sharpener
9. the book with blank pages
10. our mail carrier delivered

B Proofread the following parts of a letter for mistakes in capitalization, punctuation, and spelling. Rewrite the parts correctly.

Remember
- Capitalize the names of streets, cities, and states.
- Capitalize the first word in the greeting and closing.
- Use a comma after the greeting and the closing.
- Place a comma between the city and the state, and between the date and the year.

1. dear Uncle Bill,
2. yours truly
3. Sincerely
4. Your Freind:

5. 209 Westside street
Louisville, kentucky 40205
May 20 1985
6. Dear tracy

C Revise this first draft of a friendly letter using the directions below as a guide. Then rewrite the letter correctly on your own paper.

1. Find a sentence with slang. Write the idea in more formal language.
2. Find a sentence fragment and add words to complete it.
3. Make up and add one missing part of the heading.
4. Find and correct one capitalization error in the heading, one in line 2, and one in the closing.
5. Find and correct one punctuation error in the heading, one in the greeting, and one in line 5.
6. Find six misspelled words. Write them correctly.

2064 Maple Street

Summit   New jersey 07901

Dear Grandma

1   Ramember all those books I read last summer for the Library Story

2   Hour? I'm glad I did because our school will challenge Fairview school in a

3   Battle of the Books. We will be given questions to answer about twenty

4   books. I have bin chosen captain of our team. It'll be a real blast! I hope

5   my mind doesn't go blank? The prizes are great! A wonderfull new

6   paperback novel. If I win, I'll share my prezent with you when I visit this

7   summer. By the way, can you use the stamp on this envelop for your

8   collection?

yours truely,

Randy

Now Revise

Read your own letter to a friend. Have you used the correct letter form? Does your language fit the situation? Are your sentences complete? Now proofread for mistakes in capitalization, punctuation, and spelling. Then write your final copy in your best handwriting.

Address an envelope and mail your letter. Your friend will enjoy seeing how you are mastering the process of writing.

Handbook

I. The Structure of Words

Syllables
Base Words
Prefixes
Suffixes
Contractions
Compound Words
Abbreviations

II. The Function of Words

Nouns
Singular Nouns
Plural Nouns
Possessive Form of Nouns
Possessive Pronouns
Verbs
Past Tense Verbs
Adjectives
Adverbs

III. The Sound of Words

Vowels
Long Vowels
Short Vowels
Consonants
Silent Letters

The Structure of Words means the way words are put together.

Syllables

Words are made up of parts called syllables. The dictionary shows how words are divided into syllables.

but·ter = two syllables
dress = one syllable

Base Words

Base words are words before any changes have been made.

Base word	wrap
Base word with endings added	wrap<u>s</u> wrap<u>ped</u> wrapp<u>ing</u>
Base word with prefix added	<u>un</u>wrap

Prefixes

A prefix is a syllable added to the beginning of a word to change the meaning.

I wrapped the birthday present.
(I put the paper on the present.)

I <u>un</u>wrapped the birthday present.
(I took the paper off the present.)

I <u>re</u>wrapped the birthday present.
(I put the paper back on the present.)

Suffixes

A suffix is an ending added to a word to change
the way the word is used.

soft	The pillow is <u>soft</u>.	(adjective)
soft<u>ness</u>	The baby liked the <u>softness</u> of the pillow.	(noun)
soft<u>ly</u>	Dad <u>softly</u> sang the baby to sleep.	(adverb)
soft<u>er</u>	This pillow is <u>softer</u> than that one.	(adjective)

Contractions

A contraction is made from two words. When the two words are
put together, an apostrophe takes the place of one or more letters.

we are =	we **a**re	= we're
he will =	he **wi**ll	= he'll

Compound Words

A compound word is made from two smaller words. The
spellings do not change when the words are put together.

class + room = classroom   after + noon = afternoon

Abbreviations

An abbreviation is a way to shorten a word. Abbreviations can be
made with the first few letters of a word, followed by a period.

Wednesday Wed.   Au<u>gus</u>t Aug.   <u>inch</u> in.

Some abbreviations use the first and last letters of a word.

<u>Doctor</u> Dr.   <u>hour</u> hr.   <u>foot</u> ft.

Nouns
A noun is a word that names something.

> The <u>monkey</u> ate a <u>banana</u>.

The sentence has two words that are nouns.

Singular Nouns
A noun that names one thing is called a singular noun. The two nouns in this sentence are singular:

> The <u>monkey</u> ate a <u>banana</u>.
> (one monkey)   (one banana)

Plural Nouns
A noun that names more than one thing is a plural noun.

> The <u>monkeys</u> ate a banana.
> (more than one monkey)

> The monkey ate two <u>bananas</u>.
> (more than one banana)

Possessive Form of Nouns
The possessive form of a noun shows that something belongs to someone. Make the possessive form of a singular noun by adding **'s**.

> That car belongs to my father.
> That is my <u>father's</u> car.

When a plural noun ends in **s**, add only an apostrophe to make the possessive form.

Those uniforms belong to the players.
Those are the <u>players'</u> uniforms.

When a plural noun does <u>not</u> end in **s**, add **'s** to make the possessive form.

These toys belong to the children.
These are the <u>children's</u> toys.

Possessive Pronouns

A possessive pronoun takes the place of a noun in the possessive form.

My <u>father's</u> car = <u>his</u> car
The <u>Clark's</u> house = <u>their</u> house
<u>Ashley's</u> book = <u>her</u> book

A possessive pronoun is <u>not</u> spelled with an apostrophe.

Verbs

A verb is a word that tells about an action.

I <u>walk</u> on the beach in the summertime.
(<u>Walk</u> tells what I do.)

Past Tense Verbs

A verb that tells about an action that happened in the past is in the past tense.

We <u>walked</u> a mile to the beach.
We <u>ran</u> along the edge of the water.
(<u>Walked</u> and <u>ran</u> tell what we did.)

Adjectives

An adjective is a word that describes something.

We walked on the <u>sandy</u> beach.
(<u>Sandy</u> describes the beach.)

We ran into the <u>cold</u> water.
(<u>Cold</u> describes the water.)

Adverbs

An adverb is a word that tells how or how much.

The sailor acted <u>bravely</u> during the storm.
(<u>Bravely</u> tells how the sailor acted.)

The Sound of Words means the way you say words when you speak. Sometimes the sound will help you to spell a word.

Vowels

Five letters of the alphabet are called vowels. The vowels are **a**, **e**, **i**, **o**, and **u**.

Long Vowels

Long vowels are easy to hear because they "say their own names."

a	**e**	**i**	**o**	**u**
nation	me	fine	no	unit

Short Vowels

Short vowels sound like the vowels in these words:

a	**e**	**i**	**o**	**u**
at	ten	is	lot	up

Consonants

The consonants are all the letters of the alphabet except **a**, **e**, **i**, **o**, and **u**.

Silent Letters

Silent letters make no sound. You can see them in a word, but you cannot hear them.

Many words have a final silent **e**.

The last letter you see in the word hope is e.
The last letter you hear in the word hope is p.

Many words begin with a silent **k** or **w**.

The first letter you see in the word knee is k.
The first letter you hear in the word knee is n.

The first letter you see in the word wrist is w.
The first letter you hear in the word wrist is r.

Some words end with a silent **b**.

climb   comb   lamb

Two letters are silent in the combination **igh**.
The letters **g** and **h** make no sound.

right   high   light

How To Find a Word

A dictionary is organized like a telephone book. It lists information in alphabetical order with guide words at the top of each page.

Guide Words

The guide words help you find the right page quickly. They tell you at a glance what section of the alphabet is included on each page. The guide word on the left tells you the first word on that page. The guide word on the right tells you the last word on that page. If the word you are looking for comes alphabetically between those two words, you are on the right page.

Alphabetical Order

Alphabetical order means the order of the letters in the alphabet.

Words beginning with **a** come first.   **a**bout
Words beginning with **b** come next.   **b**ear
Words beginning with **c** come
    after words beginning with **b**.   **c**lass

When two words begin with the same letter, you must look at the second letter of each word to determine alphabetical order. When several of the letters are the same, you will have to look at the third or fourth letter to determine the alphabetical order.

toa**d**   The first three letters in the words toad and toast
toa**st**   are the same. The fourth letter must be used to determine alphabetical order. Since **d** comes before **s**, toad is alphabetized before toast.

Words Listed

The words listed in a dictionary are called entry words. A word is usually listed in its base form. Other forms of the word may be listed within the same entry.

Word Forms	Base Form	Entry Word
hurrying hurried	hurry	hurry
dances dancing	dance	dance

What the Dictionary Tells About a Word

A dictionary tells you much more than the spelling and meaning of a word. The information it contains about each word is called the entry. The parts of an entry are labeled and explained below.

The ENTRY WORD is printed in heavy black type. It is divided into syllables.

sprin·kle (spring′ k′l) *v.* to scatter in drops or bits [*Sprinkle* salt on the egg.] —**sprin′ kled, sprin′ kling**

sprout (sprout) *v.* to begin to grow [Buds *sprouted* on the roses.] —**sprout′ ed, sprout′ ing**

The RESPELLING tells you how to pronounce the word. The *Pronunciation Key* explains the respelling.

squir·rel (skwʉr′ əl) *n.* a small, bushytailed animal that lives in trees. —*pl.* **squir′ rels**

A PICTURE may be used to help you understand the meaning of the entry word.

The PART OF SPEECH is shown as an abbreviation after the pronunciation. Some words may have more than one part of speech.

stage (stāj) *n.* a platform or area on which plays, speeches, etc. are given. —*pl.* **stag′ es**

stair (ster) *n.* one of a series of steps going up or down. —*pl.* **stairs** a flight of steps.

stamp (stamp) *n.* a small piece of paper printed and sold by a government for sticking on a letter, etc. as proof that proper postage has been paid. —*pl.* **stamps**

The DEFINITION is the meaning of the word. If a word has more than one meaning, each meaning is given a number.

star (stär) *n.* a heavenly body seen as a small light at night. —*pl.* **stars** ♦*v.* to play an important part [The actress *starred* in four movies.] —**starred, star′ ring**

OTHER FORMS of the entry word are included in the same entry.

stare (ster) *v.* to look steadily at [They *stared* at his Halloween costume.] —**stared, star′ ing**

A STRESS MARK is placed after a syllable that gets an accent.

sta·tion (stā′ shən) *n.* **1** a regular stopping place for a bus or train [I'll pick you up at the bus *station*.] **2** a place that sends out radio or televison programs [WXYZ is a good radio *station*.] —*pl.* **sta′ tions**

A sample SENTENCE can help you understand the meaning of the entry word.

Pronunciation Key

SYMBOL	KEY WORDS	SYMBOL	KEY WORDS	SYMBOL	KEY WORDS
a	ask, fat	u	up, cut	n	not, ton
ā	ape, date	ʉr	fur, fern	p	put, tap
ä	car, lot			r	red, dear
		ə	a in ago	s	sell, pass
e	elf, ten		e in agent	t	top, hat
er	berry, care		e in father	v	vat, have
ē	even, meet		i in unity	w	will, always
			o in collect	y	yet, yard
i	is, hit		u in focus	z	zebra, haze
ir	mirror, here				
ī	ice, fire			ch	chin, arch
		b	bed, dub	ng	ring, singer
ō	open, go	d	did, had	sh	she, dash
ô	law, horn	f	fall, off	th	thin, truth
oi	oil, point	g	get, dog	th	then, father
oo	look, pull	h	he, ahead	zh	s in pleasure
ōo	ooze, tool	j	joy, jump		
yoo	unite, cure	k	kill, bake	'	as in (ā'b'l)
yōo	cute, few	l	let, ball		
ou	out, crowd	m	met, trim		

A heavy stress mark′ is placed after a syllable that gets a strong accent, as in **con·sid·er** (kən sid′ər).

A light stress mark′ is placed after a syllable that also gets an accent, but of a weaker kind, as in **dic·tion·ar·y** (dik′shən er′ē).

The following abbreviations are used in your dictionary for part of speech labels. They are usually shown in dark italic type.

n. noun	*pron.* pronoun	*adv.* adverb	*conj.* conjunction
v. verb	*adj.* adjective	*prep.* preposition	*interj.* interjection

The dictionary definitions used throughout this book were specially prepared by the staff of McDougal, Littell & Company and are based upon the entries in *Webster's New World Dictionary for Young Readers* with the consent of the publisher of that work, Simon & Schuster, Inc.

A

ac·tion (ak′ shən) *n.* the doing of something [There is not enough *action* in this movie.]

ad·di·tion (ə dish′ ən) *n.* an adding of numbers to get a total.

ad·ven·ture (əd ven′ chər) *n.* an exciting and dangerous happening [He told of his *adventures* in the jungle.] —*pl.* **ad·ven′tures**

age·less (āj′ lis) *adv.* seeming not to grow older [He spoke of the statue's *ageless* beauty.]

ag·ri·cul·ture (ag′ ri kul′ chər) *n.* farming.

a·head (ə hed′) *adv., adj.* in or to the front [Our car raced *ahead* of theirs. I am *ahead* of you in line.]

al·low (ə lou′) *v.* to let be done; permit [Swimming is not *allowed* here.] —**al·lowed′, al·low′ ing**

al·read·y (ôl red′ ē) *adv.* by or before this time [When we arrived, dinner had *already* begun.]

al·though (ôl tho̅′) *conj.* in spite of the fact that; even if [*Although* it's sunny, it may rain later.]

a·mount (ə mount′) *n.* **1** total [You must pay the whole *amount.*] **2** a quantity [A small *amount* of rain fell.] —*pl.* **a·mounts′**

a·muse·ment (ə myo̅o̅z′ mənt) *n.* the condition of being entertained [The clown added to our *amusement.*] —*pl.* **a·muse′ ments**

an·gry (ang′ grē) *adj.* feeling or showing anger [The *angry* man shouted at the dog.] —**an′ gri·er, an′ gri·est** —**an′ gri·ly** *adv.*

an·i·mal (an′ ə m′l) *n.* any living being that can move about by itself, has sense organs, and does not make its own food as plants do [Insects, fish, and people are kinds of *animals.*] —*pl.* **an′ i·mals**

an·kle (ang′ k′l) *n.* the joint that connects the foot and the leg. —*pl.* **an′ kles**

a·part·ment (ə pärt′ mənt) *n.* a room or rooms to live in [I live in a four-room *apartment.*] —*pl.* **a·part′ments**

ap·plaud (ə plôd′) *v.* to show approval by clapping [We *applauded* the wonderful concert.] —**ap·plaud′ ed, ap·plaud′ ing**

ap·point·ment (ə point′ mənt) *n.* an arrangement to meet at a certain time [I have an *appointment* with the dentist.] —*pl.* **ap·point′ ments**

ap·proach (ə prōch′) *v.* to come closer [She *approached* the dog nervously.] —**ap·proached′, ap·proach′ ing**

ar·range (ə rānj′) *v.* to put in a certain order [He *arranged* the living room furniture.] —**ar·ranged′, ar·rang′ ing**

a	fat	ir	here	ou	out	zh	leisure
ā	ape	ī	bite, fire	u	up	ng	ring
ä	car, lot	ō	go	ʉr	fur		a *in* ago
e	ten	ô	law, horn	ch	chin		e *in* agent
er	care	oi	oil	sh	she	ə = i *in* unity
ē	even	oo	look	th	thin		o *in* collect
i	hit	o̅o̅	tool	th	then		u *in* focus

art·ist (är′ tist) **n.** a person whose work is painting, drawing, or sculpture [The *artist* painted her portrait.] —*pl.* **art′ ists**

as·ter·oid (as′ tə roid) **n.** any of the small planets that orbit around the sun between Mars and Jupiter. —*pl.* **as′ ter·oids**

as·tro·naut (as′ trə nôt) **n.** a person trained to make rocket flights in outer space. —*pl.* **as′ tro·nauts**

at·tach (ə tach′) **v.** to fasten or join together [*Attach* the end of the rope to the boat.] —**at·tached′, at·tach′ ing**

at·ten·tion (ə ten′ shən) **n.** the act of or ability to keep one's mind on something [The principal had our *attention*.]

auc·tion (ôk′ shən) **n.** a public sale at which each thing is sold to the person offering to pay the highest price. —*pl.* **auc′ tions**

au·di·ience (ô′ dē əns) **n.** a group of persons who hear and see a speaker, play, concert, etc. [The *audience* clapped wildly.] —*pl.* **au′ di·enc·es**

au·di·to·ri·um (ô′də tôr′ē əm) **n.** a room where an audience can gather. —*pl.* **au·di·to′ri·ums**

Au·gust (ô′ gəst) **n.** the eighth month of the year [The weather gets hot in *August*.]

au·thor (ô′ thər) **n.** a person who writes a book or story. —*pl.* **au′ thors**

au·to·mat·ic (ôt′ə mat′ ik) **adj.** moving or working by itself [This pencil sharpener is *automatic*.] —**au·to·mat′i·cal·ly adv.**

au·to·mo·bile (ôt′ ə mə bēl′ *or* ôt′ ə mə bēl′) **n.** a car moved by an engine. —*pl.* **au′ to·mo·biles′**

au·tumn (ôt′ əm) **n.** the season between summer and winter; fall. —*pl.* **au′ tumns**

a·void (ə void′) **v.** to keep away from [The cat *avoids* the dog.] —**a·void′ ed, a·void′ ing**

awn·ing (ô′ ning) **n.** a covering over a window or door. —*pl.* **awn′ ings**

ax (aks) **n.** a long-handled, bladed tool for chopping wood. —*pl.* **ax′ es**

B

back·ward (bak′ wərd) **adv., adj. 1** toward the back [He turned to look *backward*.] **2** in a way opposite to the usual way [Noel is Leon spelled *backward*.]

bad (bad) **adj.** not good. —**worse, worst** —**bad′ly adv.**

badge (baj) **n.** a pin or emblem that shows one belongs to a group [She wore a police *badge*.] —*pl.* **badg′ es**

bag (bag) **n.** paper, plastic, or cloth container used for holding or carrying things [Put the groceries in the *bag*.] —*pl.* **bags**

bag·ful (bag′fool) **n.** the amount that a bag will hold [Give me a *bagful* of peanuts.] —*pl.* **bag′fuls**

band·age (ban′dij) **n.** a strip of cloth used to cover a sore or wound or to bind up an injured part of the body. ◆**v.** to bind or cover with a bandage. —**band′aged, band′ag·ing**

ban·ner (ban′ ər) **n.** a piece of cloth with an emblem or words on it; a flag.

bare·ly (ber′ lē) **adv.** only just, no more than, scarcely [It is *barely* a year old.]

base·ment (bās′ mənt) *n.* the cellar or lowest room of a building.
—*pl.* **base′ ments**

bat·ter·y (bat′ ər ē) *n.* an electric cell that makes electric current. —*pl.* **bat′ ter·ies**

bawl (bôl) *v.* to cry loudly [Our baby *bawls* all day.] —**bawled, bawl′ ing**

beach (bēch) *n.* a stretch of sand at the edge of a sea or lake. —*pl.* **beach′ es**

be·cause (bi kôz′) *conj.* for the reason that [I'm late *because* I overslept.]

been (bin) past participle of the verb **be**.

be·have (bi hāv′) *v.* to act in a proper way [Try to *behave* yourself in school.]
—**be·haved′, be·hav′ ing**

be·lieve (bə lēv′) *v.* to accept as true or real [Can we *believe* that story?]
—**be·lieved′, be·liev′ ing**

bench (bench) *n.* a long, hard seat for several persons. —*pl.* **bench′ es**

be·neath (bi nēth′) *adv., adj.* underneath [The cups are on the shelf *beneath*.] ◆*prep.* below [The ground is *beneath* my feet.]

blank (blangk) *adj.* not marked or written on [I have a *blank* piece of paper.] ◆*n.* an empty space to be written in [Fill in all the *blanks*.] —*pl.* **blanks**

blaze (blāz) *n.* a bright flame or fire.
—*pl.* **blaz′ es**

bleachers (blēch′ ərz) *n. pl.* a section of seats, usually bare benches without a roof, for watching sports.

bleed (blēd) *v.* to lose blood [The wound stopped *bleeding*.] —**bled, bleed′ ing**

blot (blät) *v.* to dry by soaking up the liquid [*Blot* the spill with a paper towel.]
—**blot′ ted, blot′ ting**

blouse (blous) *n.* a shirt worn by women and children. —*pl.* **blous′ es**

blue·ber·ry (bloo′ ber′ ē) *n.* a small, round, dark-blue berry that is eaten.
—*pl.* **blue′ber′ ries**

blur (blʉr) *v.* to make less sharp or clear [The photograph was *blurred*.] —**blurred, blur′ ring**

boil (boil) *v.* to heat liquid until it bubbles [*Boil* the soup for five minutes.] —**boiled, boil′ ing**

bone·less (bōn′ lis) *adj.* having no bones.

boss (bôs) *n.* a person who is in charge of workers. —*pl.* **boss′ es**

boul·der (bōl′ dər) *n.* a large rock made round and smooth by weather and water.
—*pl.* **boul′ ders**

bounce (bouns) *v.* to hit against a surface so as to spring back [She *bounced* the ball against the wall.] —**bounced, bounc′ ing**

branch (branch) *n.* part of a tree growing from the trunk or a limb. —*pl.* **branch′ es**

brand (brand) *n.* **1** a mark burned on the skin with a hot iron. [*Brands* were put on cattle to show who owned them.] **2** a mark or name put on the goods of a particular company; trademark. **3** a particular kind or make [This is a new *brand* of toothpaste.]

brave (brāv) *adj.* not afraid; full of courage.
—**brav′ er, brav′ est** —**brave′ ly** *adv.*

bread (bred) *n.* a common food baked from a dough. —*pl.* **breads**

a	fat	ir	here	ou	out	zh	leisure
ā	ape	ī	bite, fire	u	up	ng	ring
ä	car, lot	ō	go	ʉr	fur		a *in* ago
e	ten	ô	law, horn	ch	chin		e *in* agent
er	care	oi	oil	sh	she	ə = i *in* unity
ē	even	oo	look	th	thin		o *in* collect
i	hit	oo	tool	th	then		u *in* focus

break (brāk) *v.* to come or make come apart by force; split or crack into pieces [Don't *break* that delicate vase.] —**broke, bro′ ken, break′ ing**

breathe (brē*th*) *v.* to take air into the lungs and let it out. —**breathed, breath′ ing**

breeze (brēz) *n.* a light and gentle wind. —*pl.* **breez′ es**

bridge (brij) *n.* something built over a river, railroad, etc. to serve as a path across. —*pl.* **bridg′ es**

brief (brēf) *adj.* not lasting long [We made a *brief* visit.] —**brief′ er, brief′ est** —**brief′ ly** *adv.*

bring (bring) *v.* to carry to the place where the speaker will be [*Bring* it to my house tomorrow.] —**brought, bring′ ing**

broil (broil) *v.* to cook close to a flame or high heat [You can *broil* a steak in this oven.] —**broiled, broil′ ing**

buck·et (buk′it) *n.* a round container with a flat bottom and a curved handle. —*pl.* **buck′ ets**

buck·le (buk′ ′l) *n.* a clasp on one end of a belt or strap for fastening the other end in place. —*pl.* **buck′ les**

bud (bud) *n.* a small swelling on a plant, from which a shoot, flower, or leaves will grow. —*pl.* **buds** ♦*v.* to begin to show buds. —**bud′ded, bud′ ding**

bur·y (ber′ ē) *v.* to cover up, to hide [He *buried* the candy in his pocket.] —**bur′ ied, bur′ y·ing**

bush (boosh) *n.* a plant smaller than a tree; shrub. —*pl.* **bush′ es**

busi·ness (biz′ nis) *n.* **1** the buying and selling of goods and services. **2** a store or factory [She owns a thriving candy *business*.] —*pl.* **busi′ ness·es**

bus·y (biz′ ē) *adj.* full of activity, not idle [We were *busy* all morning.] —**bus′ i·er, bus′ i·est** —**bus′ i·ly** *adv.*

buy (bī) *v.* to get by paying money [*Buy* apples at the store.] —**bought, buy′ ing**

C

cab·in (kab′ in) *n.* **1** a small house built in a simple way, usually of wood. **2** a space on a ship or an airplane where passengers ride. —*pl.* **cab′ ins**

cam·el (kam′ ′l) *n.* a large animal with a humped back that lives in Asian and North African deserts. —*pl.* **cam′ els**

can (kan) *a helping verb used with other verbs meaning:* to know how or be able to [The baby *can* walk.] —**could**

ca·nar·y (kə ner′ ē) *n.* a small, yellow songbird. —*pl.* **ca·nar′ ies**

can·dle (kan′ d′l) *n.* a stick of wax with a wick that gives light when burned. —*pl.* **can′ dles**

cap·tain (kap′ t′n) *n.* a chief or leader of a group or activity [They saluted the *captain*.] —*pl.* **cap′ tains**

cap·ture (kap′ chər) *v.* to catch and hold by force [He *captured* the runaway dog.] —**cap′ tured, cap′ tur·ing**

care·ful (ker′ fəl) *adj.* taking care to avoid having mistakes or accidents [Be *careful* when you cross streets.] —**care′ ful·ly** *adv.*

car·pen·ter (kär′ pən tər) *n.* a worker who builds and repairs wooden things. —*pl.* **car′ pen·ters**

case (kās) *n.* a single example or happening [I had a bad *case* of the measles.] **2** a container for holding something [Be careful with the violin *case*.] —*pl.* **cas′ es**

cash·ier (ka shir′) *n.* a person who handles money in a bank, store, or restaurant.

cas·tle (kas′ ′l) *n.* a large building where a king or noble lived in the Middle Ages. —*pl.* **cas′ tles**

catch (kach) *v.* to take hold of; capture [The police *caught* the thief.] **2** to stop by grasping with the hands [Can you *catch* that football?] —**caught, catch′ ing**

cau·tion (kô′ shən) *n.* being careful to avoid danger or mistakes [Use *caution* in crossing streets.] ♦*v.* to warn [The sign cautioned us to slow down.] —**cau′ tioned, cau′ tion·ing**

ceil·ing (sēl′ ing) *n.* the top part of a room. —*pl.* **ceil′ ings**

cent (sent) *n.* a coin worth one-100th part of a dollar; penny. —*pl.* **cents**

ce·re·al (sir′ ē əl) *n.* **1** any grass that bears seeds used for food [Rice, wheat, and oats are *cereals*.] **2** food made from these seeds, especially breakfast food, as oatmeal or cornflakes. —*pl.* **ce′ re·als**

chal·lenge (chal′ ənj) *v.* to call to take part in a contest; dare [He *challenged* him to a duel.] —**chal′ lenged, chal′ leng·ing** ♦*n.* a hard task [Climbing the mountain was a *challenge*.] —*pl.* **chal′ leng·es**

chance (chans) *n.* **1** happening of events by accident [They left the future to *chance*.] **2** opportunity [This is your *chance* to succeed.] **3** a risk [Take a *chance* on winning.] —*pl.* **chanc′ es**

change·less (chānj′ lis) *adj.* remaining the same [Some people say this town is *changeless*.]

chat (chat) *v.* to talk in an easy way [The neighbors *chatted* every day.] —**chat′ ted, chat′ ting**

cheap (chēp) *adj.* **1** low in price [Vegetables are *cheaper* in summer than in winter.] **2** of low value or of poor quality [*Cheap* shoes may wear out quickly.] —**cheap′ er, cheap′ est**

chef (shef) *n.* a head cook in a restaurant. —*pl.* **chefs**

chief (chēf) *n.* the leader of a group [The police *chief* gave orders to the officers.] —*pl.* **chiefs**

child (chīld) *n.* a young boy or girl. —*pl.* **chil′ dren**

chim·ney (chim′ nē) *n.* a pipe going through a roof to carry smoke away [A wind blew over our *chimney*.] —*pl.* **chim′ neys**

choice (chois) *n.* a person or thing chosen [Smith is my *choice* for mayor.] —*pl.* **choic′ es**

cir·cus (sʉr′ kəs) *n.* a traveling show with clowns, trained animals, and acrobats. —*pl.* **cir′ cus·es**

a	fat	ir	here	ou	out	zh	leisure
ā	ape	ī	bite, fire	u	up	ng	ring
ä	car, lot	ō	go	ʉr	fur		a *in* ago
e	ten	ô	law, horn	ch	chin		e *in* agent
er	care	oi	oil	sh	she	ə =	i *in* unity
ē	even	oo	look	th	thin		o *in* collect
i	hit	ōo	tool	th	then		u *in* focus

clap (klap) *v.* to strike the hands together, as in applauding [We *clapped* when our side won.] —**clapped, clap′ ping**

claw (klô) *n.* a sharp nail on the foot of an animal or bird [The cat broke its *claw*.] —*pl.* **claws**

clerk (klʉrk) *n.* **1** an office worker who keeps records. **2** a salesperson in a store. —*pl.* **clerks**

clip (klip) *n.* anything that holds things together [I prefer a paper *clip* to a staple.] —*pl.* **clips** ◆*v.* to cut. —**clipped, clip′ ping**

clip·ping (klip′ ing) *n.* a piece cut off or out of something [Cut a *clipping* from a plant.] —*pl.* **clip′ pings**

close (klōs) *adj.* **1** with not much space between; near. **2** thorough or careful [Pay *close* attention.] —**clos′ er, clos′ est** —**close′ ly** *adv.*

clown (kloun) *n.* a person who entertains by doing comical tricks. —*pl.* **clowns**

coach (kōch) *n.* a person who trains students, athletes, singers, etc. [The swimming *coach* taught diving.] —*pl.* **coach′ es**

coil (koil) *v.* to wind around in circles or in a spiral [The sailors *coiled* the ropes.] —**coiled, coil′ ing**

coin (koin) *n.* a piece of metal money. —*pl.* **coins**

cole·slaw (kōl′ slô) *n.* a salad made of shredded raw cabbage.

com·pa·ny (kum′ pə nē) *n.* a group of people joined together in work or activity [He works for a large *company*.] —*pl.* **com′ pa·nies**

com·plete (kəm plēt′) *adj.* having no parts missing; full; whole [Her coin collection is *complete*.] —**com·plete′ ly** *adv.*

con·ceit′ ed (kən sēt′ əd) *adj.* having a high opinion of oneself.

couch (kouch) *n.* a piece of furniture for sitting or lying on; sofa. —*pl.* **couch′ es**

cough (kôf) *v.* to force air from the lungs with a loud noise [The dust made him *cough*.] —**coughed, cough′ ing**

could (kood) *past tense of* **can** [Years ago you *could* buy a hamburger for five cents.]

could·n't (kood′ 'nt) could not.

count·er (koun′ tər) *n.* a long table. —*pl.* **count′ ers**

coun·try (kun′ trē) *n.* **1** land outside of cities [Let's drive out to the *country*.] **2** the whole land of a nation [The *country* of Japan is made up of islands.] —*pl.* **coun′ tries**

cou·ple (kup′ 'l) *n.* pair [I have a *couple* of bookends.]

course (kôrs) *n.* **1** a way along which something moves. **2** one of a series of studies [I took a math *course*.] —*pl.* **cours′ es**

court (kôrt) *n.* **1** an open space with buildings or walls around it. **2** a space marked out for playing some game. **3** the palace of a king or other ruler. **4** a place where law trials are held. — *pl.* **courts**

crawl (krôl) *v.* to move by dragging the body [The baby *crawled* across the room.] —**crawled, crawl′ ing**

cray·on (krā′ ən *or* krā′ än) *n.* a small stick of chalk, charcoal, or colored wax, used for drawing or writing. —*pl.* **cray′ ons**

cream (krēm) *n.* the yellowish part of milk that contains the butterfat.

crea·ture (krē′ chər) *n.* a living being. —*pl.* **crea′ tures**

crunch·y (krunch′ ē) *adj.* making a crunching sound [Celery is *crunchy*.]

—**crunch′ i·er, crunch′ i·est**
—**crunch′ i·ness** *n.*

crutch (kruch) *n.* a support used under the arm to help in walking. —*pl.* **crutch′ es**

cub (kub) *n.* the young of certain animals. —*pl.* **cubs**

cube (kyōōb) *n.* a solid with six square, equal sides. —*pl.* **cubes**

cul·ture (kul′ chər) *n.* way of life; civilization [The *culture* of the Aztecs is interesting.] —*pl.* **cul′ tures**

cup (kup) *n.* a small container for drinking from. —*pl.* **cups**

cup·ful (kup′ fool) *n.* as much as a cup will hold [May I have a *cupful* of flour?] —*pl.* **cup′ fuls**

curl·y (kur′ lē) *adj.* full of ringlets or coils [Lambs have *curly* fur.] –**curl′ i·er, curl′ i·est**

cur·tain (kur′ tən) *n.* a piece of cloth or other material hung at a window, in front of a stage, etc., to decorate or to shut off. —*pl.* **cur′ tains**

curve (kurv) *n.* a line with no straight parts. —*pl.* **curves** ♦*v.* to turn or bend to form a curve [The road *curves* around the mountain.] —**curved, cur′ ving**

cut (kut) *v.* to divide into parts with a knife or sharp tool [Will you *cut* the cake?] —**cut, cut′ ting**

cute (kyōōt) *adj.* pretty or pleasing [What a *cute* little puppy!] —**cut′ er, cut′ est** —**cute′ ly** *adv.*

cut·ter (kut′ ər) *n.* a person or thing that cuts. —*pl.* **cut′ ters**

D

damp (damp) *adj.* slightly wet, moist.

dare (der) *v.* **1** to face bravely. **2** to challenge [She *dared* me to swim across the lake.] —**dared, dar′ ing**

daugh·ter (dôt′ ər) *n.* a girl or woman as she is related to a parent. —*pl.* **daugh′ ters**

dawn (dôn) *n.* the beginning of day [We saw the sunrise at *dawn.*]

de·fense·less (di fens′ lis) *adj.* not able to protect oneself [Without the soldiers, the town was left *defenseless.*]

def·i·ni·tion (def′ ə nish′ ən) *n.* a statement that tells what a word means [Find the *definition* in the dictionary.] —*pl.* **def′ i·ni′ tions**

de·liv·er (di liv′ ər) *v.* to bring and hand over. —**de·liv′ ered, de·liv′ er·ing**

den·tist (den′ tist) *n.* a doctor who takes care of teeth. —*pl.* **den′ tists**

de·ny (di nī′) *v.* to say that something is not true [Why *deny* the truth?] —**de·nied′, de·ny′ ing**

de·par·ture (di pär′ chər) *n.* a going away. —*pl.* **de·par′ tures**

desk (desk) *n.* a piece of furniture with a smooth top on which one can write, draw, or read. —*pl.* **desks**

de·vel·op·ment (di vel′ əp mənt) *n.* **1** the act of developing. **2** a thing that is developed. —*pl.* **de·vel′ op·ments**

a	fat	ir	here	ou	out	zh	leisure
ā	ape	ī	bite, fire	u	up	ng	ring
ä	car, lot	ō	go	ur	fur		a *in* ago
e	ten	ô	law, horn	ch	chin		e *in* agent
er	care	oi	oil	sh	she	ə = i *in* unity
ē	even	oo	look	th	thin		o *in* collect
i	hit	ōō	tool	th	then		u *in* focus

dim (dim) *adj.* not bright or clear; gloomy [It's too *dim* to see in here.] —**dim′ mer, dim′ mest** —**dim′ ly** *adv.*

dim·ple (dim′ p'l) *n.* a small, hollow spot. —*pl.* **dim′ ples**

dine (dīn) *v.* to eat dinner. —**dined, din′ ing**

di·rec·tion (də rek′ shən) *n.* the point toward which something faces [What *direction* are we going?] —*pl.* **di·rec′ tions**

dis·ap·point (dis ə point′) *v.* to fail to give or do what is expected [The team's poor playing *disappointed* the fans.] —**dis·ap·point′ ed, dis·ap·point′ ing**

dis·arm (dis ärm′) *v.* to take away weapons from [The police *disarmed* the robbers.] —**dis·armed′, dis·arm′ ing**

dis·con·nect (dis kə nekt′) *v.* to undo the connection of [Please *disconnect* the toaster.] —**dis·con·nect′ ed, dis·con·nect′ ing**

dis·hon·est (dis än′ ist) *adj.* not honest; lying, cheating [The *dishonest* clerk was fired.] —**dis·hon′ est·ly** *adv.*

dis·like (dis līk′) *v.* to have a feeling of not liking [I *dislike* rude people.] —**dis·liked′, dis·lik′ ing**

dis·loy·al (dis loi′ əl) *adj.* not loyal or faithful [The guard was *disloyal*.] —**dis·loy′ al·ty** *n.*

dis·o·be·di·ent (dis′ o·be′ di·ənt) *adj.* refusing to obey [The *disobedient* child ignored her father.] —**dis′ o·be′ di·ence** *n.*

dis·o·bey (dis ə bā′) *v.* to fail or refuse to obey [He *disobeyed* the rules.] —**dis·o·beyed′, dis·o·bey′ ing**

dis·or·der·ly (dis ôr′ dər lē) *adj.* untidy; messy [His bedroom is very *disorderly*.]

dis·play (dis plā′) *n.* showing exhibition [The *display* of jewelry is beautiful.] —*pl.* **dis·plays′**

dis·please (dis plēz′) *v.* to make angry; annoy [Her bad behavior *displeased* her grandmother.] —**dis·pleased′, dis·pleas′ ing**

dis·trust (dis trust′) *n.* a lack of trust; doubt; suspicion [His strange behavior caused *distrust*.] ◆*v.* to doubt [I *distrust* what she says.] —**dis·trust′ ed, dis·trust′ ing**

ditch (dich) *n.* trench [Be careful of the *ditch* along the road.] —*pl.* **ditch′ es**

diz·zy (diz′ ē) *adj.* having a spinning feeling that makes one unsteady [The merry-go-round made us *dizzy*.] —**diz′ zi·er, diz′ zi·est** —**diz′ zi·ly** *adv.*

doc·tor (däk′ tər) *n.* a person trained to heal the sick. —*pl.* **doc′ tors**

dodge (däj) *v.* to move quickly to one side so as to get out of the way [He *dodged* the charging goat.] —**dodged, dodg′ ing** —**dodg′ er** *n.*

does·n't (duz′ 'nt) does not.

dou·ble (dub′ 'l) *adj.* twice as much [Give me a *double* portion.] ◆*n.* **1** an amount that is twice as much. **2** a hit in baseball on which the batter gets to second base. —*pl.* **dou′ bles** ◆*v.* **1** to make twice as much. **2** to hit a double in baseball. —**dou′ bled, dou′ bling**

dough (dō) *n.* a mixture of flour, liquid, and other ingredients for baking into bread or pastry. —*pl.* **doughs**

drag (drag) *v.* to pull slowly along the ground [She *dragged* the sled upstairs.] —**dragged, drag′ ging**

draw (drô) *v.* to make a picture or design with a pencil or pen [Can you *draw* cartoons?] —**drew, drawn, draw′ ing**

dream (drēm) *n.* thoughts or feelings in the mind of a sleeping person [A bad *dream* woke her up.] ♦*v.* to have a dream [I *dreamed* I was in Africa.] —**dreamed, dream′ ing**

drench (drench) *v.* to make wet all over; soak [We were *drenched* by the rain.] —**drenched, drench′ ing**

drip (drip) *v.* to let drops of liquid fall [That faucet *drips*.] —**dripped, drip′ ping**

drown (droun) *v.* to die or kill by keeping under water. —**drowned, drown′ ing**

dust (dust) *n.* fine, powdery earth or other material that floats in the air and settles on surfaces. ♦*v.* to wipe the dust from [*Dust* the table with this cloth.] —**dust′ ed, dust′ ing**

du·ty (dōōt′ ē) *n.* any of the things to be done as a part of a person's work [These are the *duties* of a secretary.] —*pl.* **du′ ties**

E

ea·ger (ē′ gər) *adj.* anxious to do or get [We are *eager* to win.] —**ea′ ger·ly** *adv.*

ear·ly (ʉr′ lē) *adj.* soon after the start [We left in the *early* afternoon.] —**ear′ li·er, ear′ li·est**

edge (ej) *n.* the part where something begins or ends; border [We walked to the *edge* of town.] —*pl.* **edg′ es**

eight (āt) *adj.* a number, one more than seven.

el·e·phant (el′ ə fənt) *n.* a huge animal with thick skin, two ivory tusks, and a trunk. —*pl.* **el′ e·phants**

emp·ty (emp′ tē) *v.* to pour out [*Empty* the water pitcher into the sink.] —**emp′ tied,**

emp′ ty·ing ♦*adj.* having nothing in it [Don't go near the *empty* house.] —**emp′ ti·er, emp′ ti·est** —**emp′ ti·ly** *adv.*

e·nough (i nuf′) *adj.* as much as needed [There is *enough* food for all.] ♦*adv.* to the right amount [Is your steak cooked *enough*?]

en·ter·tain·ment (en′ tər tān′ mənt) *n.* something that gives pleasure [Movies are his favorite type of *entertainment*.] —*pl.* **en′ ter·tain′ ments**

en·tire·ly (in tīr′ lē) *adv.* completely.

en·vel·ope (en′ və lōp) *n.* a folded paper cover in which letters are sealed for mailing. —*pl.* **en′ ve·lopes**

e·quip·ment (i kwip′ mənt) *n.* the outfit, supplies, etc., needed for some purpose [We brought all the right camping *equipment*.]

es·cape (ə skāp′) *v.* to break loose or get free [The criminals *escaped* from jail.] —**es·caped′, es·cap′ ing**

ex·change (iks chānj′) *v.* to give in return for something else; trade [We *exchanged* telephone numbers.] —**ex·changed′, ex·chang′ ing**

ex·cite·ment (ik sīt′ mənt) *n.* anything that causes strong feeling [The burning house caused great *excitement* in town.]

a	fat	ir	here	ou	out	zh	leisure
ā	ape	ī	bite, fire	u	up	ng	ring
ä	car, lot	ō	go	ʉr	fur		a *in* ago
e	ten	ô	law, horn	ch	chin		e *in* agent
er	care	oi	oil	sh	she		ə = i *in* unity
ē	even	oo	look	th	thin		o *in* collect
i	hit	ōō	tool	th	then		u *in* focus

eye·brow (ī′ brou) **n.** the hair growing on the curved, bony part over each eye. —*pl.* **eye′ brows**

F

fact (fakt) **n.** a thing that has actually happened or that is really true [I can't deny the *fact* that I was late.] —*pl.* **facts**

fac·to·ry (fak′ tə rē) **n.** a building where goods are made [He works at a furniture *factory*.] —*pl.* **fac′ to·ries**

fair·ness (fer′ nis) **n.** justness and honesty [That judge is famous for his *fairness*.]

fam·i·ly (fam′ ə lē) **n.** a group made up of one or two parents and their children [Everyone in his *family* wears glasses.] —*pl.* **fam′ i·lies**

fan·cy (fan′ sē) **adj.** of better quality than the usual [She wore her *fancy* dress to the party.] —**fan′ ci·er, fan′ ci·est**

farm·er (fär′ mər) **n.** a person who owns or works on a farm. —*pl.* **farm′ ers**

fau·cet (fô′ sit) **n.** a device that controls the flow of liquid [Turn on the water *faucet*.] —*pl.* **fau′ cets**

fault (fôlt) **n.** blame; responsibility [It's not my *fault* we're late.] —*pl.* **faults**

fawn (fôn) **n.** a young deer. —*pl.* **fawns**

feath·er (fe*th*′ ər) **n.** any of the parts that grow out of the skin of birds. —*pl.* **feath′ ers**

fea·ture (fē′ chər) **n.** any part of the face [That girl has lovely *features*.] —*pl.* **fea′ tures**

fence (fens) **n.** a railing or wall put around a field or yard. —*pl.* **fenc′ es**

fetch (fech) **v.** to go after and bring back [The dog *fetched* my slippers.] —**fetched, fetch′ ing**

field (fēld) **n.** a piece of land having a special use, especially for growing [The farmer plowed the *field*.] —*pl.* **fields**

fierce (firs) **adj.** wild; violent [The *fierce* dog scared the campers.] —**fierc′ er, fierc′ est** —**fierce′ ly adv.**

fight (fīt) **v.** to use fists or force in trying to beat someone or something; battle [Don't *fight* with your brother.] —**fought, fight′ ing**

fit (fit) **v.** to be the right size or shape for [Does this coat *fit* you?] —**fit′ ted, fit′ ting** ◆**n.** the way something fits [This coat is a tight *fit*.]

fit·ness (fit′ nis) **n.** the state of being in good physical condition [A good diet is important to physical *fitness*.]

fix·ture (fiks′ chər) **n.** any of the fittings fastened to a building [We must fix the light *fixture*.] —*pl.* **fix′ tures**

flaw (flô) **n.** a break or scratch, that spoils something [Most diamonds have a *flaw*.] —*pl.* **flaws**

flow·er (flou′ ər) **n.** the part of a plant that bears the seed and has brightly colored petals. —*pl.* **flow′ ers**

flur·ry (flʉr′ ē) **n.** a sudden, light fall of rain or snow. —*pl.* **flur′ ries**

foil (foil) **n.** a very thin sheet of metal [Wrap it in aluminum *foil*.] —*pl.* **foils**

force·ful (fôrs′ fəl) **adj.** strong; powerful [She gave a *forceful* speech.] —**force′ ful·ly adv.**

for·ev·er (fər ev′ ər) **adv.** for all time; without ever coming to an end [No person lives *forever*.]

for·ward (fôr′ wərd) *adj.; adv.* at or toward the front. ◆*n.* a player in a front position, as in basketball or hockey. —*pl.* **for′ wards**

frac·tion (frak′ shən) *n.* a quantity less than a whole; one or more equal parts of a whole. —*pl.* **frac′ tions**

frac· ture (frak′ chər) *v.* to break or crack [He *fractured* his arm.] —**frac′ tured, frac′ tur·ing,** ◆*n.* a break or crack. —*pl.* **frac′ tures**

frame (frām) *v.* to put a border around [*Frame* the picture.] —**framed, fram′ ing**

freeze (frēz) *v.* to harden into ice; make or become solid because of cold [Water *freezes* at 0°C.] —**froze, fro′ zen, freez′ ing**

freight (frāt) *n.* a load of goods shipped [They loaded the *freight* on the train.] —*pl.* **freights**

friend·ly (frend′ lē) *adj.* showing good feelings; ready to be a friend [The big dog was not *friendly*.] —**friend′ li·er, friend′ li·est**

fringe (frinj) *n.* loose or bunches of threads used for decoration [The curtains have a *fringe*.] —*pl.* **fring′ es** ◆*adj.* additional [The company offered many *fringe* benefits.]

front (frunt) *n.* **1** the part that faces forward. **2** the beginning [That chapter is toward the *front* of the book.] —*pl.* **fronts**

fron·tier (frun tir′) *n.* the part of a country next to a wilderness [Alaska is our last *frontier*.] —*pl.* **fron·tiers′**

fudge (fuj) *n.* a soft candy.

fur·ni·ture (fur′ ni chər) *n.* the things needed for living in a house.

fu·ture (fyoo′ chər) *n.* the time that is to come [We'll buy a car sometime in the *future*.]

G

ga·rage (gə räzh′ *or* gə räj′) *n.* a closed place where automobiles are kept. —*pl.* **ga·rag′ es**

gen·tle (jent′ 'l) *adj.* **1** not rough [a *gentle* scolding]. **2** easy to handle [a *gentle* horse]. —**gen′ tler, gen′ tlest** —**gen′ tle·ness** *n.*

get (get) *v.* **1** to become the owner of by receiving, buying, etc. **2** to arrive at, reach [They *got* home early.] **3** to go and bring [*Get* your books.] —**got, got′ ten, get′ ting**

gift (gift) *n.* something given; a present. —*pl.* **gifts**

give (giv) *v.* to pass or hand over to another; to supply. —**gave, giv′ en; giv′ ing**

glad (glad) *adj.* feeling joy; happy [I'm *glad* to be here.] —**glad′ der, glad′ dest** —**glad′ ly** *adv.* —**glad′ ness** *n.*

gloom·y (gloom′ ē) *adj.* **1** dark or dim. **2** having or giving a feeling of deep sadness [He told a *gloomy story*.] —**gloom′ i·er, gloom′ i·est**

go (gō) *v.* to move along from one point to another [Time *goes* fast.] —**went, gone, go′ ing**

a	fat	ir	here	ou	out	zh	leisure
ā	ape	ī	bite, fire	u	up	ng	ring
ä	car, lot	ō	go	ur	fur		a *in* ago
e	ten	ô	law, horn	ch	chin		e *in* agent
er	care	oi	oil	sh	she	ə =	i *in* unity
ē	even	oo	look	th	thin		o *in* collect
i	hit	oo	tool	th	then		u *in* focus

goal (gōl) **n.** **1** the place at which a race is ended or at which a point is scored in certain games. **2** aim or purpose [His *goal* was to become a nurse.] —*pl.* **goals**

grab (grab) **v.** to snatch suddenly [The toddler *grabbed* the baby's toy.] —**grabbed, grab′ bing**

grace·ful (grās′ fəl) **adj.** having a beauty of form or movement [Ballet dancers are very *graceful*.] —**grace′ ful·ly adv.**

great (grāt) **adj.** fine or excellent [He gave a *great* party.] —**great′ ly adv.**

greed·y (grēd′ ē) **adj.** wanting or taking all that one can get with no thought of others' needs [The *greedy* girl ate all the cookies.] —**greed′ i·er, greed′ i·est** —**greed′ i·ly adv.**

grim (grim) **adj.** looking stern or harsh [The judge's face was *grim*.] —**grim′ mer, grim′ mest** —**grim′ ly adv.**

grip (grip) **v.** to grasp and hold fast. —**gripped, grip′ ping** ◆**n.** a grasping.

gro·cer·y (grō′ sər ē) **n.** **1** a store selling food and household supplies. **2 groceries,** *pl.* the goods sold by a grocer. —*pl.* **gro′ cer·ies**

growl (groul) **v.** to make a rumbling sound in the throat [Our dog *growled* at him.] —**growled, growl′ ing**

guide (gīd) **v.** to show the way; lead [Can you *guide* me through the museum?] —**guid′ ed, guid′ ing**

gym·nast (jim′ nast) **n.** a person trained in doing athletic exercises. —*pl.* **gym′ nasts**

H

han·dle (han′ d'l) **n.** the part by which a tool, door, cup, etc. can be held with the hand. —*pl.* **han′ dles**

hap·pi·ness (hap′ ē nis) **n.** a feeling of joy; gladness [Their laughter showed their *happiness*.]

has·n't (haz′ 'nt) has not.

haunt (hônt) **v.** to visit often [Ghosts are supposed to *haunt* old houses.] —**haunt′ ed, haunt′ ing**

have·n't (hav′ 'nt) have not.

hawk (hôk) **n.** a large bird with a strong, hooked beak and claws. —*pl.* **hawks**

ha·zy (hā′ zē) **adj.** misty or smoky [It was a *hazy* autumn day.] —**ha′ zi·er, ha′ zi·est**

head (hed) **n.** the top part of the body containing the brain and face. —*pl.* **heads**

health·y (hel′ thē) **adj.** having good health. —**health′ i·er, health′ i·est**

hedge (hej) **n.** a row of shrubs planted close together [She got scratched jumping over the *hedge*.] —*pl.* **hedg′ es**

hem (hem) **v.** to fold back the edge and sew down [Ron *hemmed* his new jeans.] —**hemmed, hem′ ming**

here's (hirz) here is.

high·way (hī′ wā) **n.** a main road. —*pl.* **high′ ways**

hinge (hinj) **n.** a joint on which a door, lid, etc. swings open and shut. —*pl.* **hin′ ges**

hoist (hoist) **v.** to lift or pull up [*Hoist* the statue into place.] —**hoist′ ed, hoist′ ing**

hol·i·day (häl′ ə dā) **n.** a day set aside to celebrate some event. —*pl.* **hol′ i·days**

home·less (hōm′ lis) *adj.* not having a home or place to live [She found a *homeless* puppy.]

hop (häp) *v.* to move by short jumps, as a bird or frog. —**hopped, hop′ ping**

hope (hōp) *v.* to have a feeling that what one wants and expects will happen [I *hope* that you win.] —**hoped, hop′ ing**

hope·ful (hōp′ fəl) *adj.* feeling or showing hope [Our team was *hopeful* about winning.] —**hope′ ful·ly** *adv.*

horse (hôrs) *n.* a large, four-legged animal with a mane and tail. —*pl.* **hors′ es**

ho·tel (hō tel′) *n.* a building where travelers may rent rooms, buy meals, etc. —*pl.* **ho·tels′**

hound (hound) *n.* a hunting dog with long, drooping ears and short hair. —*pl.* **hounds**

howl (houl) *n.* a long, wailing cry of wolves or dogs or a sound like it [The dog *howled* in pain.] —*pl.* **howls**

huge (hyōōj) *adj.* very large [Dinosaurs were *huge* creatures.] —**huge′ ly** *adv.*

I

i·cy (ī′ sē) *adj.* full of or covered with ice [Be careful of the *icy* streets.] —**i′ ci·er, i′ ci·est** —**i′ ci·ly** *adv.*

i·de·a (ī dē′ ə) *n.* something one thinks, knows, imagines; belief or thought. —*pl.* **i·de′ as**

ill·ness (il′ nis) *n.* being in poor health; sickness; disease [She took medicine for her *illness*.] —*pl.* **ill′ ness·es**

i·mag·i·na·tion (i maj′ ə nā′ shən) *n.* the power of making up ideas in the mind [In his *imagination*, he saw himself as king.] —*pl.* **i·mag′ i·na′ tions**

im·me·di·ate (i mē′ dē it) *adj.* without delay [The medicine had an *immediate* effect.] **im·me′ di·ate·ly** *adv.*

im·prove·ment (im prōōv′ mənt) *n.* a making or becoming better [Your playing shows *improvement*.] —*pl.* **im·prove′ ments**

in·com·plete (in kəm plēt′) *adj.* not complete; not whole or finished [The party would seem *incomplete* without you.] —**in·com·plete′ ly** *adv.*

in·con·sid·er·ate (in′ kən sid′ ər it) *adj.* not thoughtful of other people [Those *inconsiderate* people left their litter on the beach.] —**in′ con·sid′ er·ate·ly** *adv.*

in·cor·rect (in kə rekt′) *adj.* not correct; wrong [Your answer to the question was *incorrect*.] —**in·cor·rect′ ly** *adv.*

in·di·ges·tion (in di jes′ chən) *n.* difficulty in digesting food [The spicy meatballs gave her *indigestion*.]

in·ex·pen·sive (in′ ik spen′ siv) *adj.* not expensive; low priced [That shirt is *inexpensive*.] —**in′ ex·pen′ sive·ly** *adv.*

in·for·ma·tion (in′ fər mā′ shən) *n.* something told or facts learned; news or knowledge [An encyclopedia gives *information* about many things.]

in·ju·ry (in′ jər ē) *n.* harm done to a person or thing [She got that *injury* when she fell.] —*pl.* **in′ ju·ries**

a	fat	ir	here	ou	out	zh	leisure
ā	ape	ī	bite, fire	u	up	ng	ring
ä	car, lot	ō	go	ur	fur		a *in* ago
e	ten	ô	law, horn	ch	chin		e *in* agent
er	care	oi	oil	sh	she	ə = i *in* unity
ē	even	oo	look	th	thin		o *in* collect
i	hit	ōō	tool	th	then		u *in* focus

in·stead (in sted′) *adv.* in place of the other [Use milk *instead* of cream.]

in·struc·tion (in struk′ shən) *n.* **1** the act of teaching; education [The teacher spent his life in the *instruction* of others.] **2** something taught; lesson [I take swimming *instruction* at camp.] —*pl.* **in·struc′ tions**

in·ven·tion (in ven′ shən) *n.* something invented [The light bulb is Edison's *invention*.] —*pl.* **in·ven′ tions**

in·vite (in vīt′) *v.* to ask to be one's guest [Ten people were *invited* to the party.] —**in·vit′ ed, in·vit′ ing**

i·ron (ī′ ərn) *n.* **1** a strong metal that can be formed into various shapes after being heated. **2** a device made of metal that is heated and used for pressing clothes.

it'll (it′ ′l) it will.

J

jar (jär) *n.* a container made of glass, pottery, or stone. —*pl.* **jars**

jar·ful (jär′ fool) *n.* as much as a jar can hold [We opened a *jarful* of olives.] —*pl.* **jar′ fuls**

jer·sey (jur′ zē) *n.* a blouse, shirt, etc. made of a soft, knitted cloth. —*pl.* **jer′ seys**

jock·ey (jäk′ ē) *n.* a person who rides horses in races. —*pl.* **jock′ eys**

join (join) *v.* to become a member of [She *joined* our club.] —**joined, join′ ing**

joint (joint) *n.* a place where two bones are joined [His elbow *joint* was sore after the baseball game.] —*pl.* **joints**

jour·ney (jur′ nē) *n.* a trip. —*pl.* **jour′ neys**

judge (juj) *n.* an official who hears cases in a law court and makes decisions on them [The *judge* sentenced the guilty person.] —*pl.* **judg′ es** ◆*v.* to hear cases and make decisions in a law court [The prisoner was *judged* and sentenced.] —**judged, judg′ ing**

juic·y (joo′ sē) *adj.* full of liquid [I ate a *juicy* plum.] —**juic′ i·er, juic′ i·est**

jun·gle (jung′ g'l) *n.* land thickly covered with trees, as in the tropics. —*pl.* **jun′ gles**

K

kind·ness (kīnd′ nis) *n.* the condition of being helpful or generous [We thanked him for his *kindness*.]

L

la·dy (lā′ dē) *n.* a woman, —*pl.* **la′ dies**

lamp (lamp) *n.* a thing for giving light. —*pl.* **lamps**

lan·tern (lan′ tərn) *n.* a case of glass, paper, etc., holding a light and protecting it from wind and rain. —*pl.* **lan′terns**

late·ly (lāt′ lē) *adv.* recently.

launch (lônch) *v.* to send off into space [We saw them *launch* the rocket.] —**launched, launch′ ing**

laun·dry (lôn′ drē) *n.* clothes that have been or are about to be washed.

law (lô) *n.* any rule people are expected to obey [Is there a *law* against jaywalking?] —*pl.* **laws**

lawn (lôn) *n.* ground covered with grass that is cut short. —*pl.* **lawns**

law·yer (lô′ yər) *n.* a person whose profession is giving advice on law. —*pl.* **law′ yers**

leash (lēsh) *n.* a strap or chain to hold a dog. —*pl.* **leash′ es**

least (lēst) *adj.* smallest in size, amount, or importance [I haven't the *least* interest in the matter.]

leave (lēv) *v.* to go away or go from. —**left, leav′ing**

lec·ture (lek′ chər) *n.* a talk on a subject to an audience or class. —*pl.* **lec′ tures**

left (left) *adj.; adv.* opposite of right [Raise your *left* hand.]

leg·is·la·ture (lej′ is lā′ chər) *n.* a group of people who make laws. —*pl.* **leg′ is·la′ tures**

li·brar·y (lī′ brer′ ē) *n.* a place where books are kept for reading or borrowing [I took out four books from the *library*.] —*pl.* **li′ brar′ ies**

lie (lī) *v.* **1** to stretch one's body in a flat position. **2** to be in a flat position [The book is *lying* on the table.] —**lay, lain, ly′ ing**

like·ly (līk′ lē) *adj.* to be expected [A storm is *likely* before noon.] —**like′ li·er, like′ li·est**

limp (limp) *v.* to walk in an uneven way because of a lame leg. —**limped, limp′ ing**

line (līn) *n.* **1** a cord, rope, string, etc. **2** a wire or pipe for carrying electricity, water, gas, etc. **3** a long thin mark [Put a *line* under the correct answer.] **4** a row of persons or things [There was a long *line* of people waiting to get in.] —*pl.* **lines**

live·ly (līv′ lē) *adj.* full of energy [We have six *lively* puppies.] —**live′ li·er, live′ li·est**

lodge (läj) *n.* a small house with a special purpose [We stayed at a hunting *lodge*.] —*pl.* **lodg′ es** ♦*v.* to live at a place for a time [My brother *lodged* with my uncle when he went to college.] —**lodged, lodg′ ing**

lone·li·ness (lōn′ lē nis) *n.* unhappiness at being alone [Her *loneliness* made her cry.]

lone·ly (lōn′ lē) *adj.* unhappy at being away from friends or family [Billy was *lonely* at camp.] —**lone′ li·er, lone′ li·est**

loose (lōos) *adj.* not tight or firmly fastened [That cap is *loose*.] —**loos′ er, loos′ est** —**loose′ ly** *adv.*

lose (lōoz) *v.* **1** to fail to keep. **2** to fail to win [We *lost* the football game.] —**lost, los′ ing**

lo·tion (lō′ shən) *n.* a liquid that keeps skin soft or heals it. —*pl.* **lo′ tions**

love·li·ness (luv′ lē nis) *n.* beauty [I saw the *loveliness* of the flowers.]

love·ly (luv′ lē) *adj.* very pleasing in looks or character [The flowers were *lovely*.] —**love′ li·er, love′ li·est**

M

mag·ni·fy (mag′ nə fī) *v.* to make something seem larger than it is [The microscope *magnifies* objects fifty times.] —**mag′ ni·fied, mag′ ni·fy·ing**

a	fat	ir	here	ou	out	zh	leisure
ā	ape	ī	bite, fire	u	up	ng	ring
ä	car, lot	ō	go	ʉr	fur		a *in* ago
e	ten	ô	law, horn	ch	chin		e *in* agent
er	care	oi	oil	sh	she	ə = i *in* unity
ē	even	oo	look	th	thin		o *in* collect
i	hit	ōo	tool	th	then		u *in* focus

man (man) *n.* an adult, male human being.
—*pl.* **men**

man·u·fac·ture (man′ yə fak′ chər) *v.* to
make goods. —**man′ u·fac′ tured,
man′ u·fac′ tur·ing**

map (map) *n.* a drawing or chart of all or
part of the earth's surface. —*pl.* **maps**
◆*v.* to make a map of [Lewis and Clark
mapped western America.] —**mapped,
map′ ping**

mar·ble (mär′ b'l) *n.* **1** a kind of limestone.
2 a little ball of stone, glass, or clay. —*pl.*
mar′ bles ◆*adj.* made of marble.

march (märch) *n.* a steady walk [The
soldiers' *march* was very tiring.] —*pl.*
march′ es

match (mach) *n.* a stick of wood or
cardboard treated so it catches fire when
rubbed. —*pl.* **match′ es**

mean (mēn) *v.* to have in mind as a
purpose; intend [He *meant* to go, but
changed his mind.] —**meant, mean′ ing**

meas·ure·ment (mezh′ ər mənt) *n.* size or
amount found by using a measuring tool,
such as a yardstick [The *measurement* is
made in inches.] —*pl.* **meas′ ure·ments**

meat (mēt) *n.* the flesh of animals used as
food. —*pl.* **meats**

mer·ry (mer′ ē) *adj.* filled with fun and
laughter; cheerful [We had a *merry* party.]
—**mer′ ri·er, mer′ ri·est** —**mer′ ri·ly** *adv.*

mes·sage (mes′ ij) *n.* a piece of
information sent from one person to another
[They got a *message* by telegram.] —*pl.*
mes′ sag·es

min·i·a·ture (min′ ē ə chər) *adj.* that is a
very small copy or model [I have a
miniature railroad.]

mis·be·have (mis′ bi hāv′) *v.* to behave in
a bad way [The spoiled baby *misbehaved*.]
—**mis′ be·haved′, mis′ be·hav′ ing**

mis·con·duct (mis kän′ dukt) *n.* bad or
wrong behavior [He was accused of
misconduct.]

mis·in·form (mis in fôrm′) *v.* to give wrong
facts to [I was *misinformed* about the bus
schedule.] —**mis·in·formed′,
mis·in·form′ ing**

mis·lay (mis lā′) *v.* to put something in a
place and then forget where [I *mislaid* my
glasses.] —**mis·laid′, mis·lay′ ing**

mis·lead (mis lēd′) *v.* to lead in a wrong
direction [That old map will *mislead* you.]
—**mis·led′, mis·lead′ ing**

mis·print (mis′ print) *n.* a mistake in
printing [A *misprint* was on every page.]
—*pl.* **mis·prints′**

mis·quote (mis kwōt′) *v.* to quote wrongly.
—**mis·quot′ ed, mis·quot′ ing**

mis·read (mis rēd′) *v.* to read in the wrong
way [Did you *misread* the directions?]
—**mis·read** (mis red′), **mis·read′ ing**

mis·spell (mis spel′) *v.* to spell incorrectly
[We all *misspelled* that word.] —
mis·spelled′, mis·spell′ ing

mist (mist) *n.* a thin water vapor that can
be seen in the air and that blurs the vision
[There is a *mist* along the river bank in the
morning.]

mis·treat (mis trēt′) *v.* to treat badly.
—**mis·treat′ ed, mis·treat′ ing**

mis·un·der·stand (mis′ un dər stand′) *v.* to
understand wrong; to give a wrong meaning
to [They *misunderstood* the teacher's
words.] —**mis′·un·der·stood′,
mis′ un·der·stand′ ing**

mis·use (mis yo͞oz′) *v.* to use in a wrong way —**mis·used′, mis·us′ ing**

mix·ture (miks′ chər) *n.* something made by mixing [Punch is a *mixture* of fruit juices.] —*pl.* **mix′ tures**

mois·ture (mois′ chər) *n.* liquid causing a dampness.

mo·ment (mō′ mənt) *n.* a very short period of time [Let us pause for a *moment*.] —*pl.* **mo·ments**

mon·ey (mun′ ē) *n.* metal coins or paper bills to take the place of these issued by a government for use in buying and selling.

mop (mäp) *n.* a bundle of rags or yarn fastened to a stick used for washing floors. ◆*v.* to wash or wipe with a mop [Sailors often *mop* the deck.] —**mopped, mop′ ping**

mope (mōp) *v.* to be gloomy and dull [Rainy days make me *mope*.] —**moped, mop′ ing**

mo·tion (mō′ shən) *n.* movement [The car made a forward *motion*.] —*pl.* **mo′ tions**

moun·tain (moun′ t'n) *n.* a very high hill. —*pl.* **moun′ tains**

mul·ti·pli·ca·tion (mul′ tə pli kā′ shən) *n.* adding a figure to itself a certain number of times. —*pl.* **mul′ ti·pli·ca′ tions**

mul·ti·ply (mul′ tə plī) *v.* to repeat a figure a number of times [*Multiply* 10 by 4 to get 40.] —**mul′ ti·plied, mul′ ti·ply·ing**

must·n't (mus′ 'nt) must not.

N

na·tion (nā′ shən) *n.* a state or country. —*pl.* **na′ tions**

na·ture (nā′ chər) *n.* everything in the physical world that is not made by humans [Are you a *nature* lover?]

naugh·ty (nôt′ ē) *adj.* not behaving; disobedient [The *naughty* puppy made a mess.] —**naugh′ ti·er, naugh′ ti·est —naugh′ ti·ly** *adv.*

neat (nēt) *adj.* clean and in good order [His room was very *neat*.]

neigh·bor (nā′ bər) *n.* a person who lives by someone else [The closest *neighbor* lives three miles away.] —*pl.* **neigh′ bors**

nice (nīs) *adj.* good, pleasant, agreeable, pretty, kind, polite, etc. [That is a *nice* sweater.] —**nic′ er, nic′ est —nice′ ly** *adv.*

niece (nēs) *n.* the daughter of one's brother or sister. —*pl.* **niec′ es**

noise (noiz) *n.* sound, especially a loud sound [The *noise* of the fireworks woke up the baby.] —*pl.* **nois′ es**

nurse (nʉrs) *n.* a person trained to care for sick people and help doctors. —*pl.* **nurs′ es**

O

oc·cu·py (äk′ yə pī) *v.* to live in [They have *occupied* that house for fifteen years.] —**oc′ cu·pied, oc′ cu·py·ing**

o'clock (ə kläk′) *adv.* of the clock [It is twelve *o'clock* midnight.]

a	fat	ir	here	ou	out	zh	leisure
ā	ape	ī	bite, fire	u	up	ng	ring
ä	car, lot	ō	go	ʉr	fur		a *in* ago
e	ten	ô	law, horn	ch	chin		e *in* agent
er	care	oi	oil	sh	she	ə =	i *in* unity
ē	even	oo	look	th	thin		o *in* collect
i	hit	o͞o	tool	*th*	then		u *in* focus

of·fice (ôf′ is) **n.** the place where a certain kind of business is carried on [This is a lawyer's *office*.] —*pl.* **of′ fic·es**

of·fi·cer (ôf′ ə sər) **n.** **1** a person holding some office. **2** a member of the police force. —*pl.* **of′ fi·cers**

oil (oil) **n.** a greasy liquid that burns.

o·pin·ion (ə pin′ yən) **n.** a belief that is not based on what is certain, but on what one thinks to be likely [In my *opinion*, it will rain tomorrow.] —*pl.* **o·pin′ ions**

or·ange (ôr′ inj *or* är′ inj) **n.** **1** a round citrus fruit with a reddish-yellow skin. **2** a reddish yellow color. —*pl.* **or′ ang·es**

os·trich (ôs′ trich) **n.** a large bird of Africa and southwestern Asia with a long neck and legs. —*pl.* **os′ trich·es**

ought (ôt) *a helping verb used with infinitives and meaning:* **1** to be forced by what is right or necessary [You *ought* to apologize.] **2** likely or expected [It *ought* to be over soon.]

ounce (ouns) **n.** a unit of weight. —*pl.* **ounc′ es**

out·law (out′ lô) **n.** a criminal [The *outlaw* ran from the police.] —*pl.* **out′ laws**

P

pack·age (pak′ ij) **n.** a wrapped parcel [We got a large *package* in the mail.] —*pl.* **pack′ ag·es**

page (pāj) **n.** an entire leaf in a book, newspaper, etc. [This *page* is torn.] —*pl.* **pag′ es**

pas·ture (pas′ chər) **n.** land where grass and plants grow and where cattle, sheep, etc. can feed. —*pl.* **pas′ tures**

patch (pach) **n.** a piece of cloth, metal, etc. used to mend a hole or worn spot. ◆*v.* to put a patch on [I *patched* my old sweater.] —**patched, patch′ ing**

pause (pôz) **n.** a short stop in speech or work [He made a dramatic *pause* in his speech.] —*pl.* **paus′ es** ◆*v.* to stop for a short time [The crying baby *paused* for breath.] —**paused, paus′ ing**

pave·ment (pāv′ mənt) **n.** a paved road or sidewalk. —*pl.* **pave′ ments**

paw (pô) **n.** the foot of an animal that has claws [Our dog hurt his front *paw*.] —*pl.* **paws**

peace·ful (pēs′ fəl) **adj.** quiet; calm [They played a *peaceful* game of checkers.] —**peace′ ful·ly adv.**

peach (pēch) **n.** a round, juicy fruit with fuzzy skin. —*pl.* **peach′ es**

peak (pēk) **n.** the pointed top of a mountain [He climbed to the *peak* of the mountain.] —*pl.* **peaks**

pen·cil (pen′ s′l) **n.** a long, thin piece of wood, metal, etc. with a center stick of graphite or crayon for writing or drawing. —*pl.* **pen′ cils**

peo·ple (pē′ p′l) **n.** human beings.

pe·ri·od (pir′ ē əd) **n.** **1** a portion of time into which a game, a school day, etc. is divided. **2** the mark of punctuation used at the end of most sentences and after abbreviations. —*pl.* **pe′ ri·ods**

pick·le (pik′ ′l) **n.** a vegetable preserved in salt water, vinegar, or spicy liquid. —*pl.* **pick′ les**

pic·ture (pik′ chər) **n.** a likeness of a person, thing, or scene made by drawing, painting, or photography. —*pl.* **pic′ tures**

piece (pēs) **n.** one of a set of things [She lost a chess *piece*.] —*pl.* **piec′ es**

pi·lot (pī′ lət) **n.** a person who flies an aircraft [He wants to be a helicopter *pilot*.] —*pl.* **pi′ lots**

pine (pīn) **n. 1** an evergreen tree with cones and leaves shaped like needles. **2** the wood of this tree. —*pl.* **pines**

pitch (pich) **v.** to throw or toss [*Pitch* the garbage in the can.] —**pitched, pitch′ ing**

pit·y (pit′ ē) **n.** a feeling of sorrow for another's trouble [She felt *pity* for the caged lion.] —*pl.* **pit′ ies** ◆*v.* to feel sorrow for [They *pitied* the lost animal.] —**pit′ ied, pit′ y·ing**

plan (plan) **n.** a thought-out method of doing something [We made our vacation *plans* early.] —*pl.* **plans**

plane (plān) **n.** a man-made craft that flies through the air. —*pl.* **planes**

plant (plant) **n.** any living thing that cannot move and makes its own food by photosynthesis. —*pl.* **plants**

plate·ful (plāt′ fool) **n.** as much as a plate will hold [I ate a *plateful* of spaghetti.] —*pl.* **plate′ fuls**

pledge (plej) **n.** a promise or agreement [They said the *pledge* of allegiance to the flag.] —*pl.* **pledg′ es**

plen·ty (plen′ tē) **n.** a supply that is large enough; all that is needed [We have *plenty* of help.]

plot (plät) **v.** to plan secretly [They *plotted* to rob the bank.] —**plot′ ted, plot′ ting**

point (point) **n.** a sharp end [The needle has a sharp *point*.] —*pl.* **points** ◆*v.* to aim [The compass needle *pointed* north.] —**point′ ed, point′ ing**

poi·son (poi′ z'n) **n.** a substance that causes illness or death. —*pl.* **poi′ sons** ◆*adj.* is or contains a poison [*poison* gas].

po·lite·ness (pə līt′ nəs) **n.** the state of being polite.

porch (pôrch) **n.** an open room outside a building [We sat on the screened *porch* after lunch.] —*pl.* **porch′ es**

pos·ture (päs′ chər) **n.** the way one holds the body [Good *posture* is important.]

pound (pound) **n.** a unit of weight equal to 16 ounces [I bought a *pound* of candy.] —*pl.* **pounds**

pow·er (pou′ ər) **n.** strength or force [The *power* of the storm was frightening.] —*pl.* **pow′ ers**

pre·pare (pri par′) **v.** to get ready [He *prepared* for the test by studying hard.] —**pre·pared′, pre·par′ ing**

pres·ent (prez′ 'nt) **adj. 1** being at a certain place; not absent [Is everyone *present* today?] **2** of this time, not past or future. **n. 1** this time; now. **2** something given; gift [He gave me a *present*.] —*pl.* **pres·ents**

pres·i·dent (prez′ i dənt) **n.** the highest officer of a company, club, government, etc. —*pl.* **pres′ i·dents**

price·less (prīs′ lis) **adj.** too valuable to be measured by price [The painting is *priceless*.]

a	fat	ir	here	ou	out	zh	leisure
ā	ape	ī	bite, fire	u	up	ng	ring
ä	car, lot	ō	go	ʉr	fur		a *in* ago
e	ten	ô	law, horn	ch	chin		e *in* agent
er	care	oi	oil	sh	she	ə =	i *in* unity
ē	even	oo	look	th	thin		o *in* collect
i	hit	o͞o	tool	th	then		u *in* focus

prin·ci·pal (prin′ sə pəl) *n.* the head of a school. —*pl.* **prin′ ci·pals**

prod·uct (präd′ əkt) *n.* something produced by nature or by human beings [Wood is a natural *product*.]

prom·ise (präm′ is) *n.* an agreement to do or not to do something. —*pl.* **prom′ is·es** ◆*v.* to make a promise [I *promised* to visit her soon.] —**prom′ ised, prom′ is·ing**

proud (proud) *adj.* feeling or causing pride or pleasure [I was *proud* of my drawing.] —**proud′ er, proud′ est, —proud′ ly** *adv.*

prove (pro͞ov) *v.* to show that something is true or correct [The experiment *proved* she was right.] —**proved, prov′ ing**

prowl (proul) *v.* to roam in a secret way [Our cat *prowls* for mice.] —**prowled, prowl′ ing**

punc·tu·a·tion (pungk′ choo wā′ shən) *n.* the use of commas, periods, etc. in writing [We study *punctuation* in school.]

punc·ture (pungk′ chər) *v.* to pierce [*Puncture* the balloon.] —**punc′ tured, punc′ tur·ing**

pur·ple (pʉr′ p'l) *n.* a color that is a mixture of red and blue.

Q

ques·tion (kwes′ chən) *n.* **1** something asked [The curious girl asked a *question*.] **2** a matter to be considered; problem [It's not a *question* of money.] —*pl.*
ques′ tions ◆*v.* to ask questions of [The police officer *questioned* him.] —**ques′ tioned, ques′ tion·ing**

R

rail·way (rāl′ wā) *n.* tracks for the wheels of a train. —*pl.* **rail′ ways**

rare (rer) *adj.* not often found; not common [The zoo has many *rare* birds.] —**rar′ er, rar′ est** —**rare′ ly** *adv.*

raw·hide (rô′ hīd) *n.* a cattle hide that has been made into leather.

re·ceive (ri sēv′) *v.* to take or get what has been given or sent [He *received* many presents.] —**re·ceived′, re·ceiv′ ing**

re·fuse (ri fyo͞oz′) *v.* to say one will not take or do something [He *refused* to take his medicine.] —**re·fused′, re·fus′ ing**

rein·deer (rān′ dir) *n.* a large deer found in northern regions. —*pl.* **rein′ deer**

re·joice (ri jois′) *v.* to be or make happy [We *rejoiced* at the news.] —**re·joiced′, re·joic′ ing**

re·lief (ri lēf′) *n.* **1** a lessening of pain, discomfort, or worry [This medicine gives *relief* from coughing.] **2** help given to poor people, flood victims, etc. [The Red Cross gave *relief* after the hurricane.]

rel·ish (rel′ ish) *n.* pickles, olives, etc. —*pl.* **rel′ ish·es**

re·mem·ber (ri mem′ bər) *v.* to think of again. —**re·mem′ bered, re·mem′ ber·ing**

rent (rent) *n.* money paid at regular times for the use of a house, office, land, etc. ◆*v.* to get or give the use of a house, land, etc. in return for regular payment of money. —**rent′ ed, rent′ ing**

re·ply (ri plī′) *v.* to answer by saying something [She *replied* to the question.] —**re·plied′, re·ply′ ing**

re·port·er (ri pôrt′ ər) *n.* a person who reports news. —*pl.* **re·port′ ers**

re·trieve (ri trēv′) *v.* to find and bring back [Our dog *retrieves* balls.] —**re·trieved′, re·triev′ ing**

rip (rip) *v.* to tear apart [I *ripped* the hem of my skirt.] —**ripped, rip′ ping**

rob (räb) *v.* to steal by using force or threats [The criminals *robbed* the bank.] —**robbed, rob′ bing**

robe (rōb) *n.* a long outer garment, as a bathrobe. —*pl.* **robes** ♦*v.* to dress in a long garment [The king was *robed* in red velvet.] —**robed, rob′ ing**

rot (rät) *v.* to fall apart or spoil [A dead tree will *rot*.] —**rot′ ted, rot′ ting**

rough (ruf) *adj.* not smooth or level; uneven [The wagon ride was *rough*.] —**rough′ er, rough′ est** —**rough′ ly** *adv.*

rust·y (rus′ tē) *adj.* coated with rust. —**rust′ i·er, rust′ i·est**

S

sad (sad) *adj.* feeling unhappy [We were *sad* to see her go.] —**sad′ der, sad′ dest** —**sad′ ly** *adv.* —**sad·ness** *n.*

sad·ness (sad′ nis) *n.* the feeling of unhappiness; sorrow [The loss of his pet caused him great *sadness*.]

safe (sāf) *adj.* free from harm or danger [I feel *safe* at home.] —**saf′ er, saf′ est** —**safe′ ly** *adv.*

sail·or (sāl′ ər) *n.* an enlisted person in the navy. —*pl.* **sail′ ors**

sale (sāl) *n.* **1** the act of selling [The clerk made ten *sales* today.] **2** a special selling of goods at prices lower than usual [The store held a clearance *sale*.] —*pl.* **sales**

sam·ple (sam′ p'l) *n.* specimen or example [He showed me a *sample* of his typing.]

—*pl.* **sam′ ples** ♦*v.* to test by trying a sample [He *sampled* the grapes.] —**sam′ pled, sam′ pling**

sand·box (sand′ bäks) *n.* a box filled with sand. —*pl.* **sand′ box·es**

sand·wich (sand′ wich *or* san′ wich) *n.* slices of bread with meat, cheese, etc. between them. —*pl.* **sand′ wich·es**

sat·is·fy (sat′ is fī) *v.* to meet the needs of; to please [This meal will *satisfy* him.] —**sat′ is·fied, sat′ is·fy·ing**

sauce (sôs) *n.* a liquid or dressing used to make food tastier [Put lots of *sauce* on my spaghetti.] —*pl.* **sauc′ es**

sau·cer (sô′ sər) *n.* a small dish for a cup to rest on [She spilled coffee in the *saucer*.] —*pl.* **sau′ cers**

sau·sage (sô′ sij) *n.* meat, chopped up, seasoned, and stuffed into a tube [I like *sausage* on my pizza.] —*pl.* **sau′ sag·es**

saw·dust (sô′ dust) *n.* tiny bits of wood formed in sawing wood.

scar (skär) *n.* a mark left on the skin when a cut or burn has healed. ♦*v.* to mark with or form a scar [The cut *scarred* his knee.] —**scarred, scar′ ring**

a	fat	ir	here	ou	out	zh	leisure
ā	ape	ī	bite, fire	u	up	ng	ring
ä	car, lot	ō	go	ʉr	fur		a *in* ago
e	ten	ô	law, horn	ch	chin		e *in* agent
er	care	oi	oil	sh	she	ə =	i *in* unity
ē	even	oo	look	th	thin		o *in* collect
i	hit	o͞o	tool	*th*	then		u *in* focus

scare (sker) *v.* to make or become afraid; frighten [The mask *scared* him.] —**scared, scar′ ing**

scent (sent) *n.* a faint smell; odor [I like the *scent* of freshly cut hay.] —*pl.* **scents**

sci·en·tist (sī′ ən tist) *n.* an expert in science. —*pl.* **sci′ en·tists**

score (skôr) *n.* the number of points made in a game [Her highest bowling *score* was 110.] —*pl.* **scores** ♦*v.* to make points in a game [The hockey player *scored* two goals.] —**scored, scor′ ing**

score·less (skôr′ lis) *adj.* not having scored any points.

scrap (skrap) *n.* a small piece; bit [I dropped a *scrap* of paper.] —*pl.* **scraps**

scrape (skrāp) *v.* to scratch or rub something from. ♦*n.* a scraped place [I have a painful *scrape* on my ankle.] —*pl.* **scrapes**

scratch (skrach) *v.* to rub with fingernails to relieve itching [He *scratched* a mosquito bite.] —**scratched, scratch′ ing**

scrawl (skrôl) *v.* to write hastily [She *scrawled* a note to her friend.] —**scrawled, scrawl′ ing**

scraw·ny (skrô′ nē) *adj.* skinny. —**scraw′ ni·er, scraw′ ni·est**

scream (skrēm) *v.* to give a loud, shrill cry, as in fright or pain. —**screamed, scream′ ing** ♦*n.* a loud, shrill cry or sound. —*pl.* **screams**

scrub (skrub) *v.* to clean by rubbing hard [*Scrub* the floors.] —**scrubbed, scrub′ bing**

sec·re·tar·y (sek′ rə ter′ ē) *n.* a person whose work is keeping records, etc. for a person or organization. —*pl.* **sec′ re·tar′ ies**

sec·tion (sek′ shən) *n.* a part cut off [Eat a *section* of an orange.] —*pl.* **sec′ tions**

se·cure (si kyo͞or′) *adj.* free from fear, care, or worry; safe [I feel *secure* about my grades.] —**se·cure′ ly *adv.***

seek (sēk) *v.* to try to find [Miners went west to *seek* gold.] —**sought, seek′ ing**

sense·less (sens′ lis) *adj.* stupid, foolish, meaningless [His mumbling was *senseless*.] —**sense′ less·ly *adv.***

sen·tence (sen′ t’ns) *n.* a group of words used to tell or ask something [''I saw John '' is a *sentence*.] —*pl.* **sen′ tenc·es**

sep·a·rate (sep′ ər it) *adj.* set apart from the others; not joined [The garage is *separate* from the house.] —**sep′ a·rate·ly *adv.***

serve (surv) *v.* to offer food or drink to [The waiter *served* our dinner.] —**served, serv′ ing**

shame·ful (shām′ fəl) *adj.* bringing shame or disgrace [Stealing is *shameful*.] —**shame′ ful·ly *adv.***

shape·less (shāp′ lis) *adj.* without a well-formed shape [The old rag doll was *shapeless*.]

share (sher) *v.* to divide and give out [He *shared* his candy with his friends.] —**shared, shar′ ing** *n.* a part that each one gets [They want their *share* of the pie.] —*pl.* **shares**

shawl (shôl) *n.* a large piece of cloth worn over the shoulders. —*pl.* **shawls**

she's (shēz) **1** she is. **2** she has.

shield (shēld) *v.* to protect [Trees *shield* us from storms.] —**shield′ ed, shield′ ing**

♦**n.** armour used to ward off blows [The knight used his *shield* in battle.] —*pl.* **shields**

shine (shīn) *v.* **1** to be bright or give off light [The sun was *shining*.] **2** to make something give off light [*Shine* your flashlight under the bed.] —**shone** *or* **shined, shin′ ing**

ship (ship) *n.* any vessel, larger than a boat, for traveling on water. —*pl.* **ships** ♦**v.** to send in a ship, train, or plane [The cargo was *shipped* from New York.] —**shipped, ship′ ping**

ship·ment (ship′ mənt) *n.* goods that are shipped or transported. —*pl.* **ship′ ments**

shoot (shoot) *v.* **1** to send out with force from a gun, bow, etc. **2** to throw or send out swiftly and with force. —**shot, shoot′ ing**

should (shood) *v.* a helping verb used with other verbs when speaking of something that is likely to happen or of something that one ought to do [The show *should* begin soon. We *should* go now.]

shoul·der (shōl′ dər) *n.* the part of the body to which an arm or foreleg is connected. —*pl.* **shoul′ ders**

should·n't (shood′ ′nt) should not.

shout (shout) *v.* to speak in a loud voice [She *shouted* across the yard.] —**shout′ ed, shout′ ing**

sig·na·ture (sig′ nə chər) *n.* a person's name as he or she has written it. —*pl.* **sig′ na·tures**

sil·ly (sil′ ē) *adj.* not showing good sense [The *silly* dog barked at its reflection.] —**sil′ li·er, sil′ li·est**

sim·ple (sim′ p'l) *adj.* easy [That is a *simple* task.] —**sim′ pler, sim′ plest**

sin·cere (sin sir′) *adj.* honest; truthful; not pretending [Are you *sincere* in wanting to help?] —**sin·cer′ er, sin·cer′ est** —**sin·cere′ ly** *adv.*

sin·gle (sing′ g'l) *adj.* one only [The carriage was drawn by a *single* horse.]

sketch (skech) *v.* to make a simple drawing of [He *sketched* a picture of the house.] —**sketched, sketch′ ing**

skin (skin) *n.* **1** the tissue covering the body of persons and animals. **2** the outer covering of some fruits and vegetables. ♦**v.** to remove the skin from [I *skinned* my elbow by falling.] —**skinned, skin′ ning**

sleeve·less (slēv′ lis) *adj.* without sleeves.

sleigh (slā) *n.* a carriage with runners that moves on snow or ice. —*pl.* **sleighs**

slide (slīd) *v.* to move easily along a surface [Children *slide* on the ice.] —**slid** (slid), **slid′ ing**

slim (slim) *adj.* thin. —**slim′ mer, slim′ mest** —**slim′ ness** *n.*

smart (smart) *adj.* intelligent or clever. —**smar′ ter, smar′ test**

smudge (smuj) *n.* a dirty spot; smear. —*pl.* **smudg′ es**

snap (snap) *v.* to make a sharp, cracking sound [She *snapped* her fingers.] —**snapped, snap′ ping** ♦**n.** a fastening that closes with a clicking sound [Some jeans have a *snap* at the waist.] —*pl.* **snaps**

a	fat	ir	here	ou	out	zh	leisure
â	ape	ī	bite, fire	u	up	ng	ring
ä	car, lot	ō	go	ʉr	fur		a *in* ago
e	ten	ô	law, horn	ch	chin		e *in* agent
er	care	oi	oil	sh	she	ə =	i *in* unity
ē	even	oo	look	th	thin		o *in* collect
i	hit	o͞o	tool	th	then		u *in* focus

sneeze (snēz) *v.* to blow breath in a sudden, uncontrolled way [She *sneezed* in the dusty room.] —**sneezed, sneez′ ing** ◆*n.* an act of sneezing [Her *sneeze* was very loud.] —*pl.* **sneez′ es**

snore (snôr) *v.* to breathe noisily while sleeping [He *snored* so loudly it woke us up.] —**snored, snor′ ing**

soc·cer (säk′ ər) *n.* a football game in which a round ball is moved by kicking.

soft (sôft) *adj.* **1** not hard or firm [This pillow is *soft*.] **2** smooth [*soft* skin]. —**soft′ ly** *adv.* —**soft′ ness** *n.*

soil (soil) *n.* the top layer of earth [Cover the seeds with *soil*.] —*pl.* **soils** ◆*v.* to make or become dirty —**soiled, soil′ ing**

sore (sôr) *adj.* giving pain, aching [I have a *sore* toe.] —**sor′ er, sor′ est** —**sore′ ness** *n.*

sought (sôt) *past tense and past participle of* **seek**

sour (sour) *adj.* having the sharp taste of lemon juice or vinegar [Unripe fruit tastes *sour*.] —**sour′ ly** *adv.*

space (spās) *n.* **1** the area that contains all things in the universe [All the stars exist in *space*.] **2** the area inside of something or between things [That closet has enough *space*.] —*pl.* **spa′ ces**

speak (spēk) *v.* to say something [Please *speak* more quietly.] —**spoke, spo′ ken, speak′ ing**

spice (spīs) *n.* any vegetable substance that gives flavor or smell to food [Pepper is a useful *spice*.] —*pl.* **spices**

spi·der (spī dər) *n.* a small animal with eight legs that makes webs. —*pl.* **spi′ ders**

spin·ach (spin′ ich) *n.* a vegetable with large, dark-green leaves.

spoil (spoil) *v.* to make worthless or rotten [Ink stains *spoiled* the paper.] —**spoiled, spoil′ ing**

sponge (spunj) *n.* anything full of holes that can soak up liquid [He cleaned the counter with a *sponge*.] —*pl.* **spong′ es**

spook·y (spo͞ok′ ē) *adj.* of, like, or suggesting a ghost. —**spook′ i·er, spook′ i·est**

sprawl (sprôl) *v.* to sit or lie with arms and legs spread out. —**sprawled, sprawl′ ing**

sprin·kle (spring′ k′l) *v.* to scatter in drops or bits [*Sprinkle* salt on the egg.] —**sprin′ kled, sprin′ kling**

sprout (sprout) *v.* to begin to grow [Buds *sprouted* on the roses.] —**sprout′ ed, sprout′ ing**

squir·rel (skwur′ əl) *n.* a small, bushytailed animal that lives in trees. —*pl.* **squir′ rels**

stage (stāj) *n.* a platform or area on which plays, speeches, etc. are given. —*pl.* **stag′ es**

stair (ster) *n.* one of a series of steps going up or down. —*pl.* **stairs** a flight of steps.

stamp (stamp) *n.* a small piece of paper printed and sold by a government for sticking on a letter, etc. as proof that proper postage has been paid. —*pl.* **stamps**

star (stär) *n.* a heavenly body seen as a small light at night. —*pl.* **stars** ◆*v.* to play an important part [The actress *starred* in four movies.] —**starred, star′ ring**

stare (ster) *v.* to look steadily at [They *stared* at his Halloween costume.] —**stared, star′ ing**

sta·tion (stā′ shən) *n.* **1** a regular stopping place for a bus or train [I'll pick you up at the bus *station*.] **2** a place that sends out radio or televison programs [WXYZ is a good radio *station*.] —*pl.* **sta′ tions**

stead·y (sted' ē) *adj.* not shaky [Hold the ladder *steady*.] —**stead' i·er, stead' i·est** ◆*v.* to make or become steady [*Steady* that boat, please.] —**stead' ied, stead' y·ing,** —**stead' i·ly** *adv.*

steak (stāk) *n.* a slice of meat, especially beef [They ate sirloin *steak* for dinner.] —*pl.* **steaks**

steep (stēp) *adj.* slanting sharply up or down [That hill is very *steep*.] —**steep'er, steep'est**

step (step) *v.* to move by placing the foot forward, backward, sideways, up, or down [He *stepped* over the puddle.] —**stepped, step' ping**

stitch (stich) *v.* to see [The doctor *stitched* his cut knee.] —**stitched, stitch' ing**

sto·ry (stôr' ē) *n.* a written or spoken tale. —*pl.* **sto' ries**

stove (stōv) *n.* a device for cooking or heating by the use of gas, electricity, etc. —*pl.* **stoves**

strange (strānj) *adj.* peculiar, odd [He was wearing a *strange* costume.] —**strang' er, strang' est** —**strange' ly** *adv.*

strap (strap) *n.* a narrow strip for holding things. —*pl.* **straps**

straw (strô) *n.* a tube used for sucking a drink [I sipped a soda through a *straw*.] —*pl.* **straws**

straw·ber·ry (strô' ber' ē) *n.* a small, red, juicy fruit. —*pl.* **straw' ber' ries**

stream (strēm) *n.* a flow of water such as a small river. —*pl.* **streams** ◆*v.* to flow in a stream. —**streamed, stream' ing**

stretch (strech) *v.* to pull out to, or past, its full length [He *stretched* the rubber band until it broke.] —**stretched, stretch' ing**

stu·dent (stōōd' 'nt) *n.* a person who studies. —*pl.* **stu' dents**

stud·y (stud' ē) *v.* to read or think about so as to understand [We *studied* our lessons.] —**stud' ied, stud' y·ing**

sub·merge (səb murj') *v.* to put, go, or stay under water [Whales can *submerge* for half an hour.] —**sub·merged', sub·merg' ing**

sub·trac·tion (səb trak' shən) *n.* the act of subtracting one from another.

sub·way (sub' wā) *n.* an underground electric railway. —*pl.* **sub' ways**

sug·ges·tion (səg jes' chən) *n.* something mentioned to think over [They made a *suggestion* to improve the park.] —*pl.* **sug·ges' tions**

sup·ply (sə plī') *v.* to give what is needed [The camp *supplies* sheets.] —**sup·plied', sup·ply' ing** ◆*n.* **1** the amount at hand [I have a large *supply* of paper.] **2 supplies,** *pl.* materials [school *supplies*]. —*pl.* **sup·plies'**

sure·ly (shoor' lē) *adv.* without doubt; certainly [He will *surely* remember his promise.]

sur·prise (sər prīz') *v.* to cause one to feel wonder by being unexpected [Her sudden anger *surprised* us.] —**sur·prised', sur·pris' ing.** ◆*n.* something that is not expected [The party will be a *surprise*.] —*pl.* **sur·pris' es**

a	fat	ir	here	ou	out	zh	leisure
ā	ape	ī	bite, fire	u	up	ng	ring
ä	car, lot	ō	go	ur	fur		a *in* ago
e	ten	ô	law, horn	ch	chin		e *in* agent
er	care	oi	oil	sh	she	ə =	i *in* unity
ē	even	oo	look	th	thin		o *in* collect
i	hit	ōo	tool	th	then		u *in* focus

sur·round (sə round′) *v.* to enclose [The police *surrounded* the criminals.] —**sur·round′ ed, sur·round′ ing**

switch (switch) *v.* to shift; change [Let's *switch* the party to tonight.] —**switched, switch′ ing**

T

ta·ble (tā′ b′l) *n.* **1** a piece of furniture with a flat top set on legs [Put the dishes on the kitchen *table*.] **2** a chart of facts and figures [Study the *table* in this book.] —*pl.* **ta′ bles**

tap (tap) *v.* to hit lightly [She *tapped* my shoulder.] —**tapped, tap′ ping**

tape (tāp) *n.* a strong strip used for binding or tying. ♦*v.* to tie with tape [The doctor *taped* my bad knee.] —**taped, tap′ ing**

taste·less (tāst′ lis) *adj.* without taste or flavor [Spaghetti is *tasteless* without sauce.]

teach (tēch) *v.* to help to learn how to do something [He *taught* us to skate.] —**taught, teach′ ing**

teach·er (tēch′ ər) *n.* a person who teaches. —*pl.* **teach′ ers**

team (tēm) *n.* a group of people working or playing together. —*pl.* **teams**

tem·per·a·ture (tem′ prə chər) *n.* the degree of hotness or coldness. —*pl.* **tem′ per·a·tures**

ten·der·ness (ten′ dər nəs) *n.* the state of being soft or loving.

thaw (thô) *v.* to melt [The snow *thawed*.] —**thawed, thaw′ ing**

there's (*ther*z) there is.

they'd (*th*ād) they would.

they'll (*th*āl) they will.

they're (*th*er) they are.

they've (*th*āv) they have.

thin (thin) *adj.* **1** lean, slender. **2** not deep and strong; weak [She spoke in a *thin* voice.] —**thin′ ner, thin′ nest** —**thin′ ly adv.**

think (thingk) *v.* to believe, expect, or imagine [They *think* they can come.] —**thought, think′ ing**

thor·ough (th*u*r′ ō) *adj.* complete [Make a *thorough* search.]

though (thō) *conj.* in spite of the fact that [*Though* it rained, we went.]

thou·sand (thou′ z′nd) *n., adj.* ten times one hundred [This tree is a *thousand* years old.] —*pl.* **thou′ sands**

thread (thred) *n.* a thin cord used in sewing. —*pl.* **threads**

through (thrōō) *prep.* from side to side or end to end of [The nail went *through* the board.]

tick·le (tik′ ′l) *v.* to touch lightly, so as to cause twitching or laughter. —**tick′ led, tick′ ling**

ti·ger (ti′ gər) *n.* a large, fierce animal of the cat family, living in Asia. —*pl.* **ti′ gers**

ti·ny (tī′ nē) *adj.* very small [There is a *tiny* spot on the wall.] —**ti′ ni·er, ti′ ni·est**

tire·less (tīr′ lis) *adj.* does not become tired [She is a *tireless* worker.] —**tire′ less·ly adv.**

ton (tun) *n.* a U.S. measure of weight equal to 2,000 pounds. —*pl.* **tons**

touch (tuch) *v.* to use the hand or finger to feel something [He *touched* the wet paint.] —**touched, touch′ ing**

tough (tuf) *adj.* very difficult or hard [Shoveling snow is *tough* work.]

toward (tôrd) *prep.* in the direction of [The house faces *toward* the park.]

tow·er (tou′ ər) *n.* a building that is much higher than it is wide [The water *tower* was struck by lightning.] —*pl.* **tow′ ers**

trade (trād) *v.* to exchange [I′ll *trade* my comic books for your football.] —**trad′ ed, trad′ ing**

train (trān) *n.* a line of railroad cars pulled by a locomotive. —*pl.* **trains**

treas·ure (trezh′ ər) *n.* money or jewels collected [Pirates used to bury stolen *treasure*.] —*pl.* **treas′ ures**

treas·ur·er (trezh′ ər ər) *n.* a person in charge of a treasury. —*pl.* **treas′ ur·ers**

treat (trēt) *v.* to deal with or act toward in a certain way [*Treat* the visitors with respect.] —**treat′ ed, treat′ ing ◆** *n.* anything that gives pleasure [It was a *treat* to hear them sing.] —*pl.* **treats**

trim (trim) *v.* to make neat or tidy, especially by clipping [He *trimmed* his fingernails.] —**trimmed, trim′ ming**

trip (trip) *v.* to stumble or make stumble [She *tripped* over the rug.] —**tripped, trip′ ping**

tro·phy (trō′ fē) *n.* anything kept as a token of victory [The winning runner was given a silver *trophy*.] —*pl.* **tro′ phies**

trou·ble (trub′ ′l) *n.* a difficult or unhappy situation [We′ve never had *trouble* with our neighbors.] —*pl.* **trou′ bles**

trough (trôf) *n.* a long, narrow, open container from which animals eat or drink. —*pl.* **troughs**

tru·ly (trōō′ lē) *adv.* in fact; really [Are you *truly* sorry?]

truth (trōōth) *n.* that which is true; the real facts [Did the newspaper print the *truth* about you?] —*pl.* **truths**

try (trī) *v.* to make an effort [We must *try* to help them.] —**tried, try′ ing**

tub (tub) *n.* bathtub. —*pl.* **tubs**

tube (tōōb) *n.* **1** a long, slender, hollow piece of material [We breathe through the bronchial *tubes*.] **2** a long, slender container with a screw cap at one end. —*pl.* **tubes**

tube·ful (tōōb′ fool) *n.* a full tube of. —*pl.* **tube′ fuls**

tub·ful (tub′ fool) *n.* a full tub of. —*pl.* **tub′ fuls**

tur·tle (tur′ t′l) *n.* an animal with a soft body covered by a hard shell. —*pl.* **tur′ tles**

twin·kle (twing′ k′l) *v.* to shine with quick flashes of light; sparkle [Stars seem to *twinkle* in the sky.] —**twin′ kled, twin′ kling**

U

ug·ly (ug′ lē) *adj.* unpleasing to look at [That painting is *ugly*.] —**ug′ li·er, ug′ li·est**

a	fat	**ir**	here	**ou**	out	**zh**	leisure
ā	ape	**ī**	bite, fire	**u**	up	**ng**	ring
ä	car, lot	**ō**	go	**ur**	fur		a *in* ago
e	ten	**ô**	law, horn	**ch**	chin		e *in* agent
er	care	**oi**	oil	**sh**	she	**ə =** i *in* unity
ē	even	**oo**	look	**th**	thin		o *in* collect
i	hit	**ōo**	tool	**th**	then		u *in* focus

un·a·ware (un ə wer′) *adj.* not aware [We were *unaware* of the danger.]

un·ex·pect·ed (un′ ik spek′ tid) *adj.* not expected; surprising, sudden [The gift was *unexpected*.] —**un·ex·pec′ ted·ly** *adv.*

un·fas·ten (un fas′ ′n) *v.* to open. —**un·fas′ tened, un·fas′ ten·ing**

un·fin′ ished (un fin′ isht) *adj.* not finished or completed [The statue is still *unfinished*.]

un·fold (un fōld′) *v.* to open and spread out something that has been folded [*Unfold* the map carefully.] —**un·fold′ ed, un·fold′ ing**

un·friend·ly (un frend′ lē) *adj.* not friendly; showing bad feelings [That man seems very *unfriendly*.]

un·hurt (un hurt′) *adj.* not injured [He was *unhurt* in the fall.]

un·im·por·tant (un′ im por′ t′nt) *adj.* not important, minor [The message was *unimportant*.]

un·in·ter·est·ing (un in′ tər ist ing) *adj.* not interesting; dull [This book is very *uninteresting*.]

un·known (un nōn′) *adj.* not known, seen, or heard before [The writer of that poem is *unknown*.]

un·law·ful (un lô′ fəl) *adj.* against the law, illegal [Polluting the water is *unlawful*.] —**un·law′ ful·ly** *adv.*

un·nec·es·sar·y (un nes′ ə ser′ ē) *adj.* not necessary; needless. [His trip to the store was *unnecessary*.] —**un·nec′ es·sar′ i·ly** *adv.*

un·pop·u·lar (un päp′ yə lər) *adj.* not popular; not liked by most people [He was *unpopular* with the voters.]

un·pre·pared (un′ pri pard′) *adj.* not prepared or ready [We were *unprepared* for visitors.]

un·sat·is·fac·tor·y (un′ sat is fak′ tə rē) *adj.* not good enough to meet needs or wishes [Her work was *unsatisfactory*.] —**un′ sat·is·fac′ tor·i·ly** *adv.*

un·sel·fish (un sel′ fish) *adj.* not selfish; putting the good of others before one's own interests [His *unselfish* act was admired by others.] —**un·self′ ish·ly** *adv.*

un·til (un til′) *prep.* up to the time of [Don't leave *until* noon.] ◆*conj.* to the point that [She ate *until* she was full.]

un·u·su·al (un yoo′ zhoo wəl) *adj.* not usual or common. —**un·u′ su·al·ly** *adv.*

un·wel·come (un wel′ kəm) *adj.* not wanted [That rude person is *unwelcome* here.]

use·ful (yoos′ fəl) *adj.* that can be used [A can opener is a *useful* tool.] —**use′ ful·ly** *adv.*

V

va·ca·tion (və kā′ shən *or* vā kā′ shən) *n.* a period of time when one stops working to rest [They went to Mexico on *vacation*.] —*pl.* **va·ca′ tions** ◆*v.* to take one's vacation [We *vacationed* at home this summer.] —**va·ca′ tioned, va·ca′ tion·ing**

vi·ta·min (vīt′ ə min) *n.* any of certain substances needed by the body to keep healthy. —*pl.* **vi′ ta·mins**

voice (vois) *n.* sound made through the mouth, especially in talking [His *voice* was loud.] —*pl.* **voic′ es**

vote (vōt) *v.* to show one's decision on something by marking a ballot or raising a hand [We *voted* for club president.] —**vot′ ed, vot′ ing**

voy·age (voi′ ij) *n.* a journey by water [They went on a *voyage* around the world.] —*pl.* **voy′ ag·es**

W

wait·er (wāt′ ər) *n.* a man who waits on tables. —*pl.* **wait′ ers**

wait·ress (wā′ tris) *n.* a woman who waits on tables in restaurants. —*pl.* **wait′ ress·es**

waste·ful (wāst′ fəl) *adj.* using more than needed [Some *wasteful* people throw away good food.] —**waste′ ful·ly** *adv.*

weath·er (we*th*′ ər) *n.* the conditions outside at a particular time [We had nice *weather* today.]

we'd (wēd) we would; we had.

weigh (wā) *v.* to use scales to find out how heavy a thing is [She *weighed* the package at the post office.] —**weighed, weigh′ ing**

weight (wāt) *n.* **1** the heaviness of something [Many people worry about their *weight*.] **2** any unit of heaviness such as a pound, kilogram, etc.

when's (hwenz) when is.

where's (hwerz) where is.

wheth·er (hwe*th*′ ər) *conj.* if it is true or likely that [I don't know *whether* I can go.]

who'll (hool) who will.

wide (wīd) *adj.* great in width [The street is *wide*.] —**wid′ er, wid′ est** —**wide′ ly** *adv.*

wild (wīld) *adj.* **1** living or growing in nature; not tamed or used for farming, etc. by human beings. **2** rough, not controlled, reckless [He had a *wild* plan to get rich quickly.] —**wild′ ly** *adv.*

wise·ly (wīz′ lē) *adv.* in an informed or learned way; in a way that shows good judgment [He *wisely* decided to remain silent.]

witch (wich) *n.* a woman imagined to have magic power. —*pl.* **witch′ es**

wom·an (woom′ ən) *n.* an adult, female human being. —*pl.* **wom′ en**

won·der·ful (wun′ dər fəl) *adj.* that causes wonder; marvelous; amazing.

won't (wōnt) will not.

wood·en (wood′ 'n) *adj.* made of wood.

work·man (wʉrk′ mən) *n.* a worker; laborer. —*pl.* **work′ men**

wor·ry (wʉr′ ē) *v.* to feel or make uneasy or troubled [His sadness *worried* us.] —**wor′ ried, wor′ ry·ing**

would (wood) *v.* a helping verb used in speaking of something that depends on something else, or in asking something in a polite way [She *would* have agreed if you'd waited. *Would* you please repeat that?]

wouldn't (wood′ 'nt) would not.

wres·tle (res′ 'l) *v.* to struggle with, trying to throw or force to the ground [The boys *wrestled* until they fell.] —**wres′ tled, wres′ tling**

Y

yawn (yôn) *v.* to breathe deeply in an uncontrolled manner, as when one is tired [She *yawned* at bedtime.] —**yawned, yawn′ ing**

yield (yēld) *v.* to give the right of way to [*Yield* to traffic at the next corner.] —**yield′ ed, yield′ ing**

you'd (yood) you would; you had.

a	fat	ir	here	ou	out	zh	leisure
ā	ape	ī	bite, fire	u	up	ng	ring
ä	car, lot	ō	go	ʉr	fur	ə	a *in* ago
e	ten	ô	law, horn	ch	chin		e *in* agent
er	care	oi	oil	sh	she	ə =	i *in* unity
ē	even	oo	look	th	thin		o *in* collect
i	hit	o͞o	tool	*th*	then		u *in* focus

Lesson 1

vi

serving

inviting

Lesson 2

ly

completely

closely

sincerely

bravely

Lesson 3

le

ageless

homeless

shapeless

tireless

Lesson 4

br

bread

break

Lesson 5

oi

foil

coin

joint

voice

Lesson 6

wo
won't
wouldn't

Lesson 7

ei
weigh
neighbor
receive
ceiling

Lesson 10

ys
subways
holidays
chimneys
highways

Lesson 11

rl
curlier
curliest
earlier
earliest

Lesson 12

yi
trying
denying
replying
worrying

Lesson 13

wn
lawn
dawn
yawned

wl

shawl

crawling

gh

caught

taught

daughter

au

haunt

sauce

because

autumn

ow

howl

power

clown

flower

ou

though

should

dough

enough

br

scrubbing

grabbing

Lesson 20

ps

clips

snaps

Lesson 21

op

hoped

hopped

Lesson 22

ge

dodge

edge

sponge

garage

Lesson 23

wi

witch

sandwich

Lesson 25

re

future

picture

nature

mixture

Lesson 28

po

unpopular

unimportant

Lesson 29

mi

mislead

misspell

misprint

misunderstand

Lesson 30

ot

pilot

pilot's

Lesson 31

or

doctors

doctors'

sailors

sailors'

Lesson 32

bl

double

table

marble

Lesson 33

on

action

question

invention

caution

Lesson 34

nt

basement

pavement

amusement

excitement

ILLUSTRATIONS
Shirley Beckes: 30, 35, 84, 86, 87, 90, 91, 99, 102, 108, 109, 110, 111
Gwen Connelly: 7, 52, 53, 55, 57, 65, 69, 122, 133, 137, 138, 139, 145, 146
David Cunningham: 5
Ray Fredericks: 5, 83
Martucci Studio/Jerry Malone: 6
Diana Magnuson: 8, 12, 16, 20, 24, 28, 32, 36, 169, 171, 172, 173, 174, 175, 176, 177, 178, 179, 180, 181, 182, 183, 184, 185, 186, 187, 188, 189, 190, 191, 192, 193, 194, 195, 196, 197, 199
Ed Atchison: 9, 10, 11, 13, 14, 15, 18, 19, 23, 25, 26, 29, 34, 38, 39, 42, 115
Troy Thomas: 45
George Suyeoka: 46, 50, 54, 58, 62, 66, 70, 74
Joe Veno: 47, 60, 61, 63, 67, 68, 72, 75, 117
George Ulrich: 85, 87, 94, 95, 97, 98, 101, 103, 106, 107, 113
Yoshi Miyake: 88, 92, 96, 100, 104, 112
William P. Kaufmann: 121
Larry Frederick: 123, 124, 125, 127, 128, 129, 131, 135, 141, 143, 144, 147, 148, 149, 153
B. J. Johnson: 126, 130, 134, 142, 150

Cover Photograph: Jim Brandenburg/Woodfin Camp
Cover Design: Martucci Studio

Editorial Credits

Executive Editor, Language Arts: Carolyn McConnell

Senior Editor: Sandra Corniels

Associate Editors: Lisa Maria DeSloover, Patricia King, Carol Kalas McMullen

Project Assistance: Brown Publishing Network, Inc.

Art and Design: Chestnut House, Martucci Studio

Acknowledgments
Daily Mirror Newspaper, Ltd.: For ''My Thoughts'' by Sara Gristwood, which first appeared in the *Daily Mirror's Children's Literary Competition;* copyright © 1969. Lescher & Lescher, Ltd.: For ''Since Hanna Moved Away'' from *If I Were In Charge Of The World...and Other Worries* by Judith Viorst, published by Atheneum; copyright © 1981 by Judith Viorst. Marian Reiner: For ''Growing Up'' from *The Little Hill* Poems & Pictures by Harry Behn; copyright © 1949 by Harry Behn, copyright © renewed 1977 by Alice L. Behn, all rights reserved.